P9-BHT-557

DATE DUE

DEMCO 38-296

OTHER TITLES OF INTEREST FROM ST. LUCIE PRESS

ISO 9000: An Implementation Guide for Small to Mid-Sized Businesses

The 90-Day ISO 9000 Manual: Basics Manual and Implementation Guide

Passing Your ISO 9000/QS-9000 Audit: A Step-by-Step Guide

ISO 9000—The Blueprint (software)

QS-9000

Inside ISO 14000: The Competitive Advantage of Environmental Management

The ISO 14000 EMS Audit Handbook

Competition in the 21st Century

For more information about these titles call, fax or write:

St. Lucie Press
2000 Corporate Blvd., N.W.
Boca Raton, FL 33431-9868

TEL (561) 994-0555 • (800) 272-7737
FAX (800) 374-3401
E-MAIL: information@slpress.com
WEB SITE: http://www.slpress.com

S^t_L

THE EUROPEAN UNION DIRECTIVE SERIES
for
Medical Equipment Manufacturing and The Pharmaceutical Industry

The EU AIMD (Active Implantable Medical Device) Directive

The EU Biocides Directives

The EU Certification and Technical Standards Directives

The EU Colorant Agents for Medicinal Product and Food Directives

The EU Eco-Label Directives, Regulations and Decisions

The EU Electro-Medical Equipment Directive

The EU EMC (Electromagnetic Compatibility) Directive

The EU EMEA (European Medicine Evaluation Agency) Regulations

The EU GCP (Guidelines for Good Clinical Practices)

The EU GLP (Good Laboratory Practices)

The EU GMP (Good Manufacturing Practices)

The EU Human Medicinal Products: Directives, Opinions and Regulations

The EU Human Medicinal Products Testing Directives

The EU IVD: The Proposal for the In-Vitro Diagnostic Directive

The EU Labeling of Medicinal Product Directives

The EU Liability and Product Safety Directives

The EU Low Voltage Directive

The EU Machinery Directive

The EU MDD (Medicinal Device Directive)

The EU Modules for Conformity Assessment Directives

The EU Packaging Directives

The EU PEA (Equipment Used in Potentially Explosive Atmospheres) Directive

The EU Risks Assessment: Directives and Regulations

The EU Special Medicinal Products Directives

The EU Veterinary Medicinal Product Testing Directives

The EU Video and Display Equipment Directive

The EU VMP (Veterinary Medicinal Products) Directives

The EU Worker's Safety: Physical Hazards Directive

The EU Worker's Safety: Work Equipment Directives

EU DIRECTIVE HANDBOOK

**UNDERSTANDING THE
EUROPEAN UNION COMPLIANCE PROCESS
AND WHAT IT MEANS TO YOU**

ALLEN R. BAILEY
MELINDA C. BAILEY

$S{}^t_L$

St. Lucie Press
Boca Raton, Florida

Riverside Community College
Library
4800 Magnolia Avenue
Riverside, California 92506

.98

MAY

KJE 6569 .B35 1997

Bailey, Allen R.

EU directive handbook

Copyright ©1997 by St. Lucie Press

All rights reserved. No part of this publication may be reproduced, stored in a retrieval system or transmitted in any form or by any means, electronic, mechanical, photocopying, recording or otherwise, without the prior written permission of the publisher.

Printed and bound in the U.S.A. Printed on acid-free paper.
10 9 8 7 6 5 4 3 2 1

ISBN 1-57444-102-7

All rights reserved. Authorization to photocopy items for internal or personal use, or the personal or internal use of specific clients, is granted by St. Lucie Press, provided that $.50 per page photocopied is paid directly to Copyright Clearance Center, 222 Rosewood Drive, Danvers, MA 01923 USA. The fee code for users of the Transactional Reporting Service is ISBN 1-57444-102-7 2/97/$100/$.50. The fee is subject to change without notice. For organizations that have been granted a photocopy license by the CCC, a separate system of payment has been arranged.

The copyright owner's consent does not extend to copying for general distribution, for promotion, for creating new works, or for resale. Specific permission must be obtained from St. Lucie Press for such copying.

Direct all inquiries to St. Lucie Press, Inc., 2000 Corporate Blvd., N.W., Boca Raton, Florida 33431-9868.

Phone: (561) 994-0555
E-mail: information@slpress.com
Web site: http://www.slpress.com

S^{t}L

Published by
St. Lucie Press
2000 Corporate Blvd., N.W.
Boca Raton, FL 33431-9868

Contents

Preface

With the changing nature of business in Europe, it is essential that companies understand compliance in the European Union. The EU compliance process is being adopted as the world standard. In order to remain competitive in the global marketplace, a business must meet the standards of the EU.

A great deal of time has been devoted to complying with the EU standards—but the EU Directives have been overlooked. The EU Directives are the actual laws from which standards flow. If a conflict or question arises, the directive is the source for the answer.

This book provides a general overview of the compliance process in the EU. It is a general guide for all regulated manufacturing and service fields. Section I describes the history and development of the European Union, including its philosophy, its organization, and an overview of the EU Directives. Section II outlines the benefits and liabilities of compliance to the EU Directives. Section III outlines the "how" of the compliance process. It is a step-by-step guide to obtaining the CE Marking.

The information presented in this book was obtained directly from the directives themselves, as well as numerous conversations with EU Notified Bodies and EU compliance experts.

Acknowledgment

This book could not have been written
without the love and support of Janet Bailey.
Without her patience, this project would not have been possible.

About the Authors

Allen R. Bailey is a Canadian Standards Board Registrar with over 30 years experience in manufacturing. He is a consultant and trainer in quality control and product compliance and a leading expert in the United States on EU Directives. Mr. Bailey is registered with the International Register for Assessors of Quality Systems, the Canadian Standards Board, and TASA (Technical Advisory Service for Attorneys). He is a graduate of California State University and holds masters degrees from Marshall University and Virginia Tech. He has taught polymer science and materials engineering at Penn State University.

Melinda C. Bailey studied technical writing and editing for three years at New Mexico Institute of Mining and Technology. She then went on to graduate cum laude from Harrisburg Area Community College as a Registered Nurse. This provides her a unique insight into the medical manufacturing field. Ms. Bailey has edited and written over 60 books in the medical and electronic fields. She is also an active public speaker on compliance in the European Union.

Ms. Bailey spent over seven years in the U.S. Army Reserve in communications. Recently, she received her commission as a Second Lieutenant. While in the Army, she earned several commendations, including Honor Graduate from Platoon Leadership Development Course and the Army Achievement Medal. Ms. Bailey has also won awards for her artistic and public speaking abilities.

Section I

What?

An explanation of the history
and organization of the EU

The Formation of the EU

For 50 years, the countries of Europe have been discussing becoming one economic, cultural, and monetary union. These discussions have finally crystallized into the European Union (EU). Europe has formed a common economic market. This is the largest market in the world, making up 40% of the world's gross national product and one-fifth of the total global trade in goods.* It is now possible to conform to one set of laws (called *directives*) and market a product in all the countries of Europe. As the regulatory process is finalized, compliance to the EU Directives will become absolutely necessary to sell in Europe. Products not in compliance are already being withdrawn from the market and refused entry into the EU. **Understanding the EU Directives is essential to maintaining world market share.** The EU Directives are emerging as the world standard. Already over 70 countries have adopted at least some of the directives. By the year 2000, approximately one-third of all countries will have harmonized their laws with the EU Directives. Maintaining international competitiveness will depend upon your understanding the EU Directives.

History of the European Union

The European Union is made up of 15 Member States united by the aim of protecting the health and safety of their citizens, fostering the free movement of goods, and providing for a common foreign policy and security. The formation of the EU has taken almost 50 years, starting with the Treaty of Brus-

---

* These figures are from The European Union and World Trade (p. 5), a pamphlet put out by Office for Official Publications of the European Communities.

EU Expansion Kept Canada from Adding Jobs

OTTAWA — Canada has lost out on about 50,000 jobs as trade with the European Union continues to falter, according to a new Canadian Senate report.

When the EU enlarged from nine members to 15 in 1995, Canadian exports to the EU fell from 12.4 percent of total exports to 6.4 percent. Imports from the EU, meanwhile, fell from 13.3 percent to 10 percent.

"If Canada had maintained its share of the EU market at 1988 levels, there would have been 50,000 more jobs for Canadians in 1994, based on additional exports of $4.6 billion," the report said. The report concluded that plans to further enlarge the EU to include Eastern European countries "threatens both Canadian exports and economic well-being."

"The EU's economic and political leverage will grow in relation to that of Canada as the union absorbs up to 13 more countries. The growing imbalance of power will place Canada in an increasingly more disadvantageous bargaining position."

The 12 member Senate committee undertook the study out of concern that Canadian relations with the EU might drift and deteriorate once the European nations unite in 1999. A proposal for a Transatlantic Free Trade Agreement that would include Canada in any trade relationship between the United States and the EU—made by Canada's former trade minister Roy MacLaren—was well received by Britain and Germany. But enthusiasm for it was muted by France and the United States.

The report strongly recommended that the federal government continue to press the EU and the United States to broaden their bilateral trade negotiations to include Canada.

It warns that otherwise, the United States, with its greater political and economic clout, could negotiate better access to the EU than Canada. That would make the United States more attractive than Canada for European investment, the report concluded.

In the first five months of this year, Canadian exports to the United States rose 4.7 percent to $88.2 billion, compared with a 1.8 percent increase to $6.5 billion in Canadian exports to the EU in the same period.

So far this year, Canadian imports from the United States rose only 0.7 percent, to $71.3 billion, compared with a 1.6 percent drop, to $8.1 billion, in imports from the EU, according to Statistics Canada.

Reprinted with permission from Roland Blassnig, News Ottawa Bureau. Published in *The Buffalo News*, July 21, 1996.

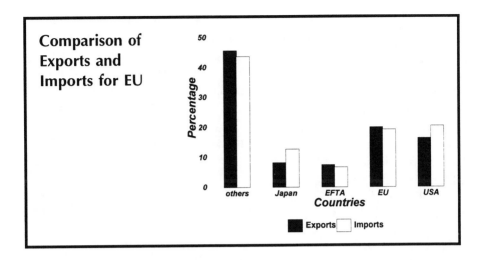

Comparison of Exports and Imports for EU

Countries

■ Exports □ Imports

The Member States

	Abbreviation
Austria	AT
Belgium	BL
Germany	DE
Denmark	DK
Greece	EL
Spain	ES
Finland	FS
France	FR
United Kingdom	UK
Ireland	IE
Italy	IT
Portugal	PT
Sweden	SE
Luxembourg	L
Netherlands	NL

The abbreviation is used in approval symbols within the EU.

sels on March 17, 1948, which was last amended on October 23, 1954. The Treaty of Brussels formed the Community to establish the European Pharmacopoeia. Signatories agreed to adopt the European Pharmacopoeia for medicinal products. This treaty formed the basis for the idea that the countries of Europe could function as one.*

On April 18, 1954, Belgium, the Federal Republic of Germany, France, Italy, Luxembourg, and the Netherlands signed the European Coal and Steel Community (ECSC), under the leadership of French Foreign Minister Robert Schuman. This treaty formed the European Community and was the start to strengthening the social ties, raising the standard of living, and promoting the harmonious development of social services in the respective countries.

* Besides the 15 members of the EU, another 24 countries have signed on to adopt the European Pharmacopoeia.

Prior to this, France had begun an initiative known as the Pléven Plan, which was supposed to unite the defense forces of Europe. This became known as the European Defense Community (EDC). However, in August 1954, the French National Assembly failed to ratify the treaty. The French felt that the EDC limited their sovereignty too much. This led to a period of inaction in progress toward a united Europe. In June 1955, the original six members of the ECSC met at the Messina Conference. They decided to focus on economic rather than military unity. This led to the signing of the European Atomic Energy Commission (EUROATOM) and the European Economic Community (EEC) in March 1957.

In 1959, the European Free Trade Area (EFTA) was formed. EFTA was comprised of the United Kingdom, Norway, Sweden, Denmark, Austria, Portugal, Iceland, and Switzerland. Finland did not officially join, but became an associate member instead. EFTA's goals were purely economic. Member nations did not wish to reduce cultural and social barriers, but only the barriers to the free movement of goods.

The United Kingdom quickly realized that there were greater benefits to joining the EC* than being a member of the EFTA. Therefore, in August 1961, it applied for membership, along with Denmark, Norway, and Ireland. However, the French distrusted the British, and General de Gaulle blocked their application in both 1961 and 1967. No headway was made until General de Gaulle stepped down in 1969. The Accession Treaties were signed on January 22, 1972 and, after ratification, went into effect on January 1, 1973. Norway was the only country unable to obtain the votes necessary for ratification; 53.49% of its citizens voted not to join the EC. As a result of the Accession Treaties, the EC's membership rose from six members to nine.

Greenland was included as a territory of Denmark. However, continuing membership in the EC was defeated in a vote in 1973. Even though the treaty has no provisions for withdrawal, Greenland became an associated overseas territory in 1985.

During the 1970s, much time was devoted to the Tindemans Report, written by Belgian Prime Minister Leo Tindemans. At that time, he was the president of the EC Council. This report proved to be too ambitious a plan, envisioning completion of the Union by 1980. Even though it failed to make the transition into a treaty, it did inject an air of renewed enthusiasm, which had been missing during the 1960s.

There were also three areas in which tangible progress was made. First, the

---

*The European Community (EC) is the original name of the EU.

European Political Cooperation (EPC) was signed. This was an agreement in which the members of the EC agreed to cooperate on foreign policy. It is still in force today. Second, the European Monetary System (EMS) was set up in March 1979. The EMS, which will continue to function until the single European currency goes into effect, is designed to control wild fluctuations in currency values. The EMS has been very effective in maintaining the stability of the Member States' currency values. Third, free trade agreements were signed with the remaining members of EFTA in 1972.*

The early 1980s was marked by intense debate over what form the Union should take. This culminated in the signing of the Draft Treaty Establishing the European Union on February 14, 1984 by the EC Parliament. It was not ratified by the Member States, but it did provide a cohesive blueprint from which the EC could work.

The draft treaty provided impetus to the Member States at the Fontainebleau and Milan Summits held in June of 1984 and 1985. They set up a committee on institutional affairs, chaired by Irish Senator James Dooge. This committee was designed to make recommendations to improve European cooperation. A committee was also set up under Pietro Adonnino. Its job was to make recommendations on ways in which the EC could be more responsive to the needs of its citizens. Its scope of action was to cover areas such as education, health, and law.

On January 1, 1981, Greece became the tenth member of the EC. Spain and Portugal became the eleventh and twelfth members in June 1985. The unification of Germany in 1990 only required minor adjustments rather than a full-scale accession treaty.

The rise of Japan as a world economic power forced the Member States to take decisive action on the formation of a workable economic union. They were quickly loosing ground in international economic markets and realized that they had to combine in order to stay competitive. On July 1, 1987, the Single European Act went into effect. This act laid the foundation for a single market by 1992. It also set up a legal framework which required Member States to cooperate on foreign policy under the EPC. Cooperation had been voluntary until the act was signed.

In 1988, the heads of state began an initiative to move the EC toward an Economic and Monetary Union (EMU). The EC was suffering from chronic unemployment, and the hope was that the EMU would help solve this. The

---

* The remaining members of EFTA were Sweden, Switzerland, Austria, Finland, Portugal, Norway, and Iceland.

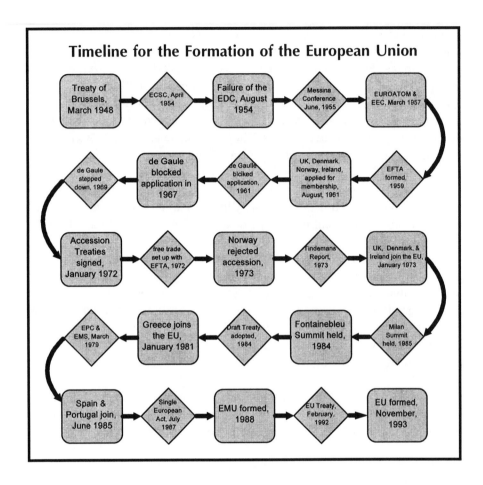

purpose of this program was to provide fixed currency rates across the borders of the Member States. It also was the beginning of a single European currency.

On February 7, 1992, the European Union Treaty was signed in Maastricht.* It went into effect on November 1, 1993, and the modern European Union was born. The struggle for ratification by the Member States was difficult and did result in some changes in the treaty, but it still made its deadline of November 1, 1993.

Meanwhile, Austria, Sweden, and Finland applied for membership. They became members in 1994. This brought the total membership to 15. Switzer-

---

* The European Union Treaty is sometimes referred to as The Maastricht Treaty.

land, Turkey, Cyprus, and Malta have all applied for membership, but negotiations continue.

Poland, the Czech Republic, the Slovak Republic, Hungary, Bulgaria, and Romania have all expressed a desire to join. However, the EU requires that its members meet a minimum industrial and economic level. These countries do not yet meet this level, but association agreements were signed with the EU in 1992 and 1993.

With Austria, Sweden, and Finland joining the EU, the final members of the EFTA became the European Economic Area (EEA).* The EEA still plays an active role in the EU. It adopts all of the EU Directives and is actively involved in the writing of standards for the EU. If you comply with the EU Directives, you can also market your product within the EEA.

Free Movement of Goods

The first major pillar of the EU is the concept of free movement of goods. One of the major reasons the Member States have banded together is to gain greater economic power. The first step toward this is to enable goods to pass freely from one Member State to another.

The concept of free movement of goods traveled a rocky road until it finally came into being in the 1990s. There was much disagreement between the states over what kinds of goods could move freely and how they could do so. In 1979, the courts issued a ruling that put an end to much of the debate. In the case of *Cassis de Dijon*, the Court of Justice ruled that a Member State could not limit the free movement of goods unless the product endangered the health and safety of its citizens, the environment, public morality, safety, the protection of national treasures, or the protection of personal or commercial property. The case involved the marketing of liqueurs in Germany. The alcohol content of Cassis de Dijon liqueur was lower than what was designated by German law to be called a liqueur. The court ruled that Germany could not restrict the marketing of the product as a liqueur merely on the basis of its alcohol content. Germany had to allow the free movement of goods.

This led to the "New Approach Directives." These directives only apply to products that are considered a risk to health, safety and the environment. They are written to be general, leaving the specifics to standards bodies such as CEN or ISO.

---

* The members of the EFTA are Switzerland, Norway, Iceland, and the Principality of Liechtenstein.

Non-regulated products (not covered by a directive) continue to fall under national regulations. These national regulations must be mutually recognized among the individual Member States. This allows the Member States a great deal of freedom but continues to ensure the free movement of goods.

Taxation has also been harmonized to ensure the free movement of goods. The EU has set up maximum import and export tariffs between the Member States and third countries.* The individual Member States are free to charge lower tariffs but they may not charge higher ones. "There are no longer any customs or tax barriers or regulations restricting the activities of individuals or the free movement of services or capital [among the EU Member States]."**

Protection of Citizens

The second pillar of the EU is the protection of its citizens. In terms of the EU, this not only means physical protection, but also protection of its citizens' rights. The EU is endeavoring to provide equality for the citizens of all its Member States.

In 1968, the Council issued a regulation ensuring the rights of workers throughout the EU. This regulation guaranteed equal wages, working conditions, and terms of employment. It also guaranteed geographical and occupational mobility and a minimum level of social integration in any Member State where a worker chooses to work. The founders of the EU felt this was essential if a united Europe was to function. Originally, this regulation only applied to gainfully employed workers, but in 1990 several directives were passed which extended this right to students, pensioners, and the unemployed if they had the economic means to support themselves and adequate healthcare coverage.

The EU is working on a program to provide mutual recognition of vocational training and college degrees. It has already succeeded in doing this for the healthcare profession. Nurses, midwives, doctors, and veterinary surgeons may practice in any Member State without retaking exams or training. The EU hopes to eventually extend this right to all training. In 1988, the EC did begin a program allowing for the mutual recognition of all higher level academic degrees greater than three years. Because of the differences in educational

---

* Third country is the term the EU uses to designate countries which are not members of either the EU or the EEA.

** Quoted from *Europe in 10 Points* (p. 30), published by the Office for Official Publications of the European Communities.

requirements, an individual may still have to take an aptitude test or an alignment course. In 1992, a similar program for trades was suggested. This program is not yet in place, but it should be soon.

Economic and Social Growth

The final pillar of the EU is to provide for economic and social growth. The EU intends to protect its home markets and increase opportunities for expansion. The results of these policies can already be seen. For instance, in the medical device field, 65% of all products sold in the EU are produced by U.S. manufacturers. The EU intends to decrease this number by at least 20% by the year 2000 and subsequently increase the number of medical devices sold within the EU that are manufactured by EU companies. This goal will probably be surpassed.

Social growth is viewed as increasing opportunities for citizens. The EU hopes to increase its citizens' standard of living. As the benefits of the common market begin to show, this goal will also be reached. The common market is too new for individual citizens to gain much at this point. However, the various EU industries are already feeling the benefits of decreased international competition and increased access to markets within the EU and the EEA. It will not be long before this translates into increased jobs and wages. As the economic benefits of the EU translate into a higher standard of living, support for the union will grow.

The European Union is now a reality. It may never become a true cultural and monetary union, but the economic union is already a reality. The EU Directives are already shaping world compliance and will continue to do so. With the globalization of the marketplace, it was inevitable that a common form of compliance would be developed and applied. The EU method of simplifying laws so that they do not have to be updated to address changes in technology makes sense, especially in light of the speed with which science is leaping ahead. The EU Directives will be the world standard. Companies can move ahead with the EU or find themselves out of the race. Global competitiveness is the only way to be truly successful in today's business world.

2

Organization of the EU

The EU is a democracy. The original founders of the EU chose the West German government as a model. There is no separation of governmental powers in the EU, as there is in the United States. Frequently the same individual belongs to different governmental bodies. It is not unusual for a law (known as a directive) in the EU to be written, reviewed, passed, and regulated by the same individuals. The European practice is based on the theory that the experts in a given field are best qualified to process a directive.

There are several important legislative bodies within the EU, the most important of which is the Commission.*

The Commission

The Commission,** headquartered in Brussels, is the executive branch of the EU. It is an impartial body that is responsible for ensuring that the provisions of the treaties are met by the individual Member States. It can refer cases to the courts or can impose penalties on individuals or companies if they are in violation of the treaties. The Commission also manages the Standing Committees of the directives and handles the day-to-day operation of the EU. "Without the 20 men and women who are its Members and the 15,000 staff who serve it, the Union would not work. The Council and the European Parliament need a proposal from the Commission before they can pass legislation, EU laws are mainly upheld by Commission action, the integrity of the single market is

---

* The concept of separation of powers is an American government concept. However, even in the United States, the FDA, for example, writes and enforces regulations.
** The Guide to EU Institutions, EU Office of Publications (EU-OP), 1996.

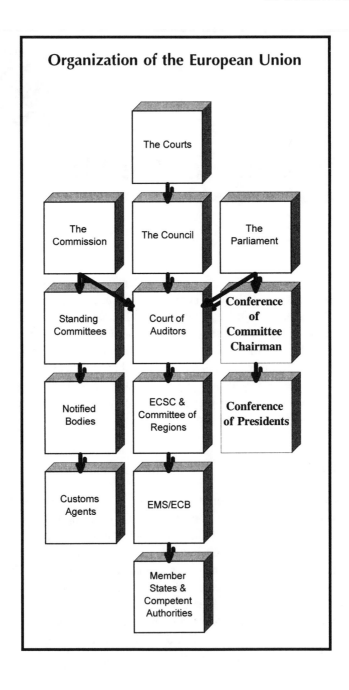

Organization of the European Union

European Commission

Number of Members—20

Number per Country—Two from France, Germany, Italy, Spain, and the United Kingdom and one from each of the other Member States

Term of Office—Five years (1995–2000)

---

preserved by Commission policing, agricultural and regional development policies are sustained, managed and developed by the Commission as is development cooperation with the countries of central and eastern Europe, Africa, the Caribbean and Pacific. Research and technological development programs vital for the future of Europe are orchestrated by the Commission."*

The EU Treaty requires that some acts, such as directives, have the consent of the Council. However, the Commission has the sole right to initiate legislation. The Commission also gives final approval to all directives in the EU. It is made up of two members and two alternates appointed by each Member State. Under the EU Treaty, appointments to the Commission must be approved by Parliament. The Commission votes are weighted the same as the Council. Most decisions of the Commission are passed by a majority of 62 votes; however, withdrawal of market approval can be passed by a simple majority vote.

The Commission is divided into 26 Directorates-General (DGs), with an additional 15 or so specialized services. Each DG is headed by a Director

---

Passing a Measure

1. If a measure receives 62 votes from the Commission, it is passed.

2. If a measure fails to obtain 62 votes, the Commission can submit the measure to a second Council discussion. It passes if representatives of three Member States with at least one-tenth of the weighted vote are in favor. This is known as the Rule of Tenths.

3. Some acts of the EU Treaty require a unanimous vote; however, a member state can abstain from voting. An abstention is not counted as a negative vote. An example of this is the Single Currency Act.

---

* The Guide to the EU Institutions, EU-OP, 1996.

EU Commission Directorates-General

DG I	External Economic Relations
DG IA	External Political Relations
DG IB	External Relations
DG II	Economic and Financial Affairs
DG III	Industrial Affairs
DG IV	Competition
DG V	Employment, Industrial Relations, and Social Affairs
DG VI	Agriculture
DG VII	Transport
DG VIII	Development
DG IX	Personnel and Administration
DG X	Audiovisual, Information, Communication, and Culture
DG XI	Environment, Nuclear Safety, and Civil Protection
DG XII	Science, Research and Development—Joint Research Center
DG XIII	Telecommunications, Information Market, and Exploitation of Research
DG XIV	Fisheries
DG XV	Internal Market and Financial Services
DG XVI	Regional Policies
DG XVII	Energy
DG XVIII	Credit and Investment
DG XIX	Budgets
DG XX	Financial Control
DG XXI	Customs and Indirect Taxation
DG XXII	Education, Training, and Youth
DG XXIII	Enterprise Policy, Distributive Trades, Tourism, and Cooperatives
DG XXIV	Consumer Policy Service

Treaty Agencies

ECHO (European Community Humanitarian Office)

EUROATOM Supply Agency

Office for Official Publications of the EU

European Foundation for the Improvement of Living and Working Conditions

European Centre for the Development of Vocational Training (Cedefop)

General, who reports to a Commissioner who has the political and operational responsibility for the work of the DG. The 26 DGs handle the day-to-day administration of specific areas. They function like departments in the United States. For example, there is a DG for agriculture. The EU Treaty gave the Commission the power to form the DGs. Each Standing Committee has a staff which operates under one of the DGs. The technical directives, such as the *Medical Device Directive*, fall under DG IV.

One of the primary functions of the DGs is to publish draft directives for public comment and review. They also are responsible for disseminating information on reported non-compliances to the Member States and maintaining surveillance reports. This is done electronically, and results can be in the hands of the Member States within five working days. Their final duties involve providing staffing to the Council.

The Council

The Council* of the European Union, usually known as the Council of Ministers, has no equivalent anywhere in the world. The Council legislates for the Union, sets its political objectives, coordinates national policies, and resolves differences between Member States and with other institutions. Under Article D of the EU Treaty,** the Council is defined as the legislative body which provides political impetus and guidelines for the EU. Under this authority, the Council initiates new policies, arbitrates internal disputes, and determines foreign policy. The main EU Council is made up of the head of state and the secretary of state from each Member State. The Member States take turns heading the EU Council for six months.

Council of the European Union

Members—Ministers of the 15 Member States

Presidency—From July 1, 1995 rotates every six months in the following sequence: Spain, Italy, Ireland, Netherlands, Luxembourg, United Kingdom, Austria, Germany, Finland, Portugal, France, Sweden, Belgium, Spain, Denmark, Greece

Meeting Place—Brussels, except in April, June, and October, when all Councils take place in Luxembourg

---

* The Guide to EU Institutions, EU-OP, 1996.
** The EU Treaty is sometimes referred to as the Maastricht Treaty.

Weighted Voting System of the Council	
Belgium	5
Denmark	3
Germany	10
Greece	5
Spain	8
France	10
Ireland	3
Italy	10
Luxembourg	2
Netherlands	5
Austria	4
Portugal	5
Finland	3
Sweden	4
United Kingdom	10

The Council meets twice a year. At these meetings, the budget and policy initiates are written. Under the EU Treaty, all minutes of meetings, including this meeting, must be approved by Parliament.

There are permanent members of the EU Council. They form the Permanent Representatives Committee, chaired by the Coreper, who serves as the Member States' ambassador to the Union. This committee sets up the individual work groups responsible for making specific preparations for initiating policies and for studying specific matters.

Unlike any institution in the United States, the composition of the Council changes depending upon the topic. The membership of the EU Council is always the heads of state and the secretaries of state. However, that is not the only council. There is a council in charge of each directive. Each Member State provides two representatives and two alternates. As an example, the *Medical Device Directive* was written by the Competent Authorities of the Member States acting under the authority of the Council.* However this council is not the same as the council that is made up of the heads of state. To further confuse the issue, they are all referred to as "the Council." The chairman is usually an appointed member of the Commission. The number of yes votes necessary to pass legislation varies with the issue being discussed (see sidebar for specifics).

---

* From The Guide to EU Institutions, EU-OP, 1996: "The Council has the characteristics of both a supranational and intergovernmental organization, deciding some matters by qualified majority voting, and others by unanimity. In its procedures, its customs and practices, and even in its disputes, the Council depends on a degree of solidarity and trust which is rare in relations between states. In 1994, the Council held around 100 formal ministerial sessions during which it adopted about 300 regulations, 50 directives and 160 decisions."

Votes Necessary to Pass a Measure

1. Sixty-two yes votes are necessary on issues submitted to the Council by the Commission (usually directives).

2. Sixty-two votes in favor, cast by at least ten members, are required for legislation written by the Council.

3. In other business matters, such as withdrawing market approval, a simple majority of the members is all that is necessary.

Parliament

The parliament is democratically elected by citizens of the EU. There are 626 members. Members are elected to five-year terms and organized into political parties.

The Members elect a president, 14 vice-presidents, and 5 quaestors. The Conference of Committee Chairmen prepares the agendas for the parliamentary committees. The Conference of Presidents maintains relationships with parliaments of countries that are not members of the EU and with international organizations. The Conference of Committee Chairmen also coordinates the work with the Council, Commissions, and the Standing Committees.

The EU Treaty expanded the powers of Parliament from budgetary matters to approving the appointment of members of the Commission, approving directives, and approving cooperation in the fields of justice and foreign policy.

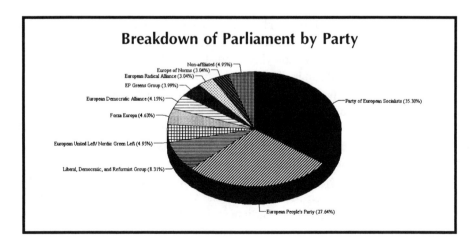

Breakdown of Parliament by Party

Non-affiliated (4.95%)
Europe of Norms (3.04%)
European Radical Alliance (3.04%)
EP Greens Group (3.99%)
European Democratic Alliance (4.15%)
Forza Europa (4.63%)
European United Left/ Nordic Green Left (4.95%)
Liberal, Democratic, and Reformist Group (8.31%)
Party of European Socialists (35.30%)
European People's Party (27.64%)

Parliament Membership

Germany	99	Portugal	25
France	87	Sweden	22
Italy	87	Austria	21
United Kingdom	87	Denmark	16
Spain	64	Finland	16
Netherlands	31	Ireland	15
Belgium	25	Luxembourg	6
Greece	25	**Total**	**626**

The members are elected every five years, with the next election to be held in 1999.

Meeting Places

- Strasbourg for monthly plenary sessions
- Brussels for committee meetings and additional sessions

The Secretariat General is based in Luxembourg

The Parliament now has final approval of the EU budget and discharge of funds. As a result of these changes, the EU is becoming more democratic and its policy-making process is beginning to be opened up to the public. As the EU progresses, the public will gradually gain more access to the institutional processes.

The public is allowed to attend some parliamentary meetings, but many are closed and the minutes are not publicized. All Parliament votes are open to the public. The EU citizenry is applying a great deal of pressure on the EU Parliament to open all meetings. This will probably occur soon.

For certain important decisions, the Council must obtain the permission of the Parliament. These areas are international agreements, accession of new members, procedures for election to Parliament, approval of all directives, and other areas that directly impact the rights of citizens.

The EU institutions operate under consultation procedures. Passage of a directive requires an opinion from the Parliament before a legislative proposal from the Commission can be adopted by the Council. This allows Parliament to approve proposed legislation. Parliament cannot normally initiate directives;

however, the *Certification and Technical Standards Directive* (94/10/EC) was initiated by Parliament. This directive transferred the power of approval of products from the Competent Authorities of the Member States to the Standing Committees. Based on this directive, the Court of Justice has ruled that the national courts cannot hear cases involving EU-regulated products.

The Courts

The court system of the EU consists of the Court of Justice and the Court of First Instance.* The role of the courts is to ensure that the treaties are correctly interpreted and the laws are properly obeyed. The Court of Justice can decide that a Member State has failed to fulfill an obligation of the treaties and require that the Member State take the necessary steps to comply. The Court can also impose a fine or penalty payment. At the request of a national court, Member State, or citizen, the Court can rule on the validity or interpretation of a Community institution or legislation. The driving force behind the common market has been the rulings of the courts. Individual citizens are taking their Member States to court over restrictions imposed on the freedom of movement of goods. It is the courts that have forced the Member States to deregulate telecommunications, reform the Custom Union, and issue the harmonized directives.

The Courts of the European Communities

Court of Justice—15 judges and 9 Advocates General

Court of First Instance—15 judges

Members of both Courts are appointed by the Member States for renewable terms of six years

---

The Court of First Instance

The Court of First Instance rules on cases brought by individuals and businesses. Withdrawal of market authorizations, permission to place on the market, decisions, and Competent Authority rulings are handled by the Court of First Instance. Its rulings can be appealed to the Court of Justice, but *the appeal can only be based on points of law*. Their are 15 judges on the Court of First

---

* The Guide to EU Institutions, EU-OP, 1996.

Instance; they serve six-year terms. Judges are appointed by agreement among the Member States.

The Court of Justice

The Court of Justice is the highest court in the EU. It decides appeals on points of law. If a national court or the Court of First Instance cannot decide on points of law, the case is appealed to the Court of Justice. It handles cases brought by Member States. "The Court of Justice may sit in plenary session or in chambers of three or five judges. It sits in plenary session when it so decides or if a Member State or an EU Institution which is a party to the proceedings so requests."* Plenary sessions are sessions in which all 15 judges hear a case. They usually involve questions concerning critical treaty issues.

There are 15 members on the Court of Justice. They serve six-year terms and are appointed by agreement among the Member States.

The European Court of Auditors

The 15 members of the European Court of Auditors audit the European financial institutions and transactions. They are appointed by a unanimous decision of the EU Council, with the approval of Parliament. The Court elects a Primus Inter Pares from among its members, who serves as the president.

The EU Treaty granted extensive powers to the Court of Auditors to examine the expenditures of the Community institutions as well as the soundness of their financial management. The Court carries out audits and has the power to execute spot checks in the EU or outside of it. It has the power to audit any business that has a contract with the EU without prior approval by the Commission.

The Court also prepares an annual report to Parliament. This is the key document which influences Parliament to approve the budget. The Court functions like the U.S. Congressional Office of the Budget and will render an opinion on a specific question. The Court's opinion is compulsory in cases of legislation of a financial nature or expenditures. Furthermore, the Court must issue a report to the Council and Parliament to assure the Member States of the financial soundness of the EU. The Court reviews the expenditures and budgets of each Directorate-General each year.

---

*The Guide to EU Institutions, EU-OP, 1996.

The Economic and Social Committee

The Economic and Social Committee (ESC)* is made up of 222 members and alternates from social and economic groups from the Member States. Members of this committee are known as counsellors, and each member serves a four-year term. The members are divided into three groups. The first group represents employers. The second group represents workers. The final group is a catchall group. It represents farmers, craftsman, small and medium-size manufacturers, the professions, consumers, scientists, teachers, cooperatives, families, and the environment. The ESC renders opinions on legislation and must be consulted by the Council, Commission, and Parliament on social and economic issues. While its Opinions are not binding, they are

> ### Economic and Social Committee
>
> **Members**—222
>
> **Breakdown of Members**—France, Germany, Italy, and the United Kingdom 24 each; Spain 21, Belgium, Greece, the Netherlands, Portugal, Sweden, and Austria 12 each; Denmark, Ireland, and Finland 9 each; Luxembourg 6
>
> **Term of Office**—Four years
>
> **Meeting Place**—Brussels, monthly

published in the *Official Journal of the European Communities*. The courts have used these Opinions in their Decisions. These Opinions are usually considered seriously by the Commission, Council, and the Parliament. Voting is done by a simple majority.

Twice a year, the ESC holds a forum to review progress on the common market. The forum enables the ESC to act as a watchdog. These forums bring attention to things left undone, foot-dragging by institutions and Member States, and draws attention to misinterpretations likely to close down markets and prevent the free circulation of goods, capital, services, and people. These forums also seek to develop consent and recommend solutions to Community decision-makers.

The Committee of the Regions

The Committee of the Regions* is made up of 222 members and an equal number of alternates who are elected from local and regional governments.

---

* The Guide to EU Institutions, EU-OP, 1996.

Committee of the Regions

Members—222

Breakdown of Members—France, Germany, Italy, and the United Kingdom 24 each; Spain 21; Austria, Belgium, Greece, the Netherlands, Portugal, and Sweden 12 each; Denmark, Finland, and Ireland 9 each; Luxembourg 6

Term of Office—Four years

Meeting Place—Brussels, five plenaries per year

They serve four-year terms. This committee contains key local politicians, and their opinions are given a great deal of weight by the Parliament, Council, and Commission. All the local infrastructure programs originate from and are supervised by this committee. Public utilities, regional development, land utilization, energy, education programs, and funding are reviewed by this committee.

The purpose of this committee is to increase grass roots involvement in the key policies of the EU. The EU Treaty created the concept of *subsidiarity*—"that decisions should be taken by those public authorities which stand as close to the citizen as possible." The primary responsibility of this committee is to provide a voice for the citizens of the EU.

The European Investment Bank

The European Investment Bank (EIB) provides loans and guarantees for large-scale public works projects. Its primary purpose is to finance investments which further EU interests. It mainly finances projects to develop trans-European transportation and telecommunications projects, protect the environment, ensure the availability of energy products, and increase the competitiveness of EU businesses. It also lends funds to its associate countries for the same purposes.

It is a non-profit lender in that it passes on its loan rates to its customers. It obtains low-interest loans on the capital markets and in turn lends this money to borrowers.

The European Monetary Institute and European Central Bank

The EU has authorized a single currency and banking system to start in 1997 with a deadline of 1999. These deadlines are set by the EU Treaty. The European Monetary Institute has been functioning since 1994, laying the groundwork for a single currency. Because of political situations, this deadline will probably not be met. It is not even possible to predict whether or not a single currency will ever be available. As economic unity progresses, there will probably be an evening out of currency rates from country to country within the EU. Regardless, the EU common market will only move forward.

Standing Committees

Under the EU Commission, each directive has a Standing Committee. The Standing Committee is responsible for approving and supervising the harmonizing of standards, Commission Decisions of Standards, Notified Bodies, and market authorizations. The draft of any proposed directive or amendment is reviewed by the Standing Committee, and in most cases the Commission will respect its findings. The Standing Committees meet with the standards organization twice a year to monitor and facilitate progress. Standing Committees are chaired by a member of the Commission, who does not have the power to vote. The Standing Committee members are usually also members of the Council that drafted and passed the directive. They are normally the Competent Authorities of the individual Member States.

Agencies

For certain areas with multiple directives, the Commission may set up an agency such as European Agency for Evaluation of Medicine (EAME). The agency then takes over the management and regulatory functions of the Commission. Agencies are granted the full powers of the Commission and act on behalf of the Commission. They can withdraw market authorizations, impose fines, review all relevant records, set fees, and keep surveillance records.

Competent Authorities

Competent Authorities (also called National Authorities) are departments of the Member States' governments which regulate a particular market sector. They are equivalent to the U.S. Food and Drug Administration or Department of Agriculture. They nominate and authorize the Notified Bodies for each directive. They monitor compliance, work on harmonizing standards, and issue individual product standards (B1 standards). The head of the Competent Authority for each Member State's Bureau of Standards is a member of the EU *Certification and Technical Standards Directive* (83/189/EEC) Standing Committee. 83/189/EEC is the primary directive for establishing the regulatory protocols.

3

The Directives

The technical directives incorporate and outline the EU regulatory procedures. The goal of a directive is to protect public health and safety and standardize the protocols for placing a product on the market. The directives are the actual laws of the EU. The Member States agree to transpose their regulations and laws, to comply with the directives, and to recognize the CE Marking. They can erect no roadblocks to the free movement of goods. The goal of free movement of goods is over 90% complete. To quote the 12th Annual Commission Report:

> To summarize the result of the Commission's work under Article 169, in 1994, it commenced 974 infringement proceedings (compared with 1209 in 1993), issued 546 reasoned opinions (compared with 352 in 1993) and refereed 89 cases to the Court of Justice (compared with 44 in 1993). These figures indicate steady progress is being made on the implementation of the EU Directives. The majority of infringements are the result of failure to notify national measures implementing Directives. While the Member States have improved the adoption of transposal measures, there is a failure as a result of a breakdown in the implementation process.

This is remarkable considering that the Commission issued over 60 new directives, including the *Low Voltage Directive* and the new *Certification and Technical Standards Directive* and *Risks Assessment Directive*. The Member States are 91.89% in compliance on transposing all the technical directives. This is very rapid progress considering the number of key directives that were passed in 1994. The *Medical Device Directive* and the *Active Implantable Medical Device Directive* were not passed by the European Parliament until the

Definitions

Annexes—The sections of a directive that are optional unless stated in an article or selected by a company.

Article—The statements in a directive that are legally binding.

CE Marking—A blanket mark stating that a product meets all the EU regulatory requirements.

Competent Authority—A national committee of a member country that determines non-compliance of products and processes.

Conformity Assessment—The formal verification that a product or service complies with the relevant directive.

Decision—A ruling by the Commission, Council, or Parliament that is legally binding.

Directive—The actual laws of the EU.

Harmonized Standard—A technical specification that has been adopted by the Standing Committee. It states the protocols that must be followed to demonstrate compliance.

Notified Body—A government-sanctioned organization that can certify a quality system or product to determine that it meets EU requirements. It is a registrar or a certified body.

Opinion—A finding by the Commission, Council, or Parliament. Opinions are non-binding but are often used by the Courts and regulatory officials in interpreting directives.

Recitals—The introductory statements that are not legally binding but show the intent of the directive and list the relevant references.

Regulation—An order by the Commission, Council, or Parliament. Orders take effect 20 days after passing, while decisions and directives will usually have a transition period.

Standing Committee—The committee formed to regulate and implement a directive.

Technical Construction File (TCF)—A document filed by a manufacturer to establish that its product is in compliance with EU Directives.

end of 1993. The electrical directives were passed in 1994. For the most part, the technical directives and decisions were completed by the July 1, 1994 deadline.

A number of problems still exist. The slow progress of the Courts was addressed by the Commission, which informed the EU Courts in July 1994 to apply Article 171 of the EU Treaty and start imposing fines for non-compliance. The Courts are starting to follow the recommendations of the Commission and impose fines. A medical device non-compliance can result in withdrawal of a product from the market and a 100,000 DM fine in Germany to a 10,000 £ fine and six months in prison in England.

The greatest progress has been made in the area of the free movement of goods. The Custom Union is fully functional. The removal of technical barriers to trade is mostly complete. Some 468 individual directives are in force, and only 4 are awaiting passage (see Table 3.2). Essentially all the planned technical directives were passed in 1994 except the *In-Vitro Diagnostic Directive*. The medicinal directives present the most problems. The new European Agency

Table 3.1   Implementation*

Member States	Applicable on Dec. 31, 1994	Directives Transposed	Compliance (%)
Belgium	1213	1088	89.7
Denmark	1213	1184	97.6
Germany	1216	1107	91.0
Greece	1214	1053	86.7
Spain	1214	1108	91.2
France	1214	1120	93.3
Ireland	1213	1115	91.9
Italy	1213	1072	88.4
Luxembourg	1213	1137	93.7
Netherlands	1213	1137	93.7
Portugal	1213	1171	96.5
United Kingdom	1213	1084	89.4

Note: In the EU Accession Treaty which added Austria, Norway, and Sweden, most of these directives were implemented.

* Twelfth Annual Review of Community Law (95/C 254/01).

Table 3.2   Technical Compliance

%

Member States	Medicinal (32 Dir.)	Technical* (90 Dir.)	Motor Vehicle (167 Dir.)	Telecom. (6 Dir.)
Belgium	78.00	96.00	93.00	83.00
Denmark	90.00	100.00	99.00	100.00
Germany	75.00	96.00	96.00	100.00
Greece	78.00	94.00	94.00	67.00
Spain	71.00	95.00	99.00	100.00
France	68.00	96.00	91.00	100.00
Ireland	71.00	96.00	97.00	67.00
Italy	84.00	96.00	94.00	100.00
Luxembourg	75.00	95.00	97.00	67.00
Netherlands	71.00	95.00	99.00	100.00
Portugal	69.00	96.00	94.00	100.00
United Kingdom	75.00	98.00	96.00	100.00
Average	77.86	96.57	96.03	95.14

* The technical directives are electrical, machinery, measuring equipment, medical, personal protection equipment, pressure vessels, gas-fired appliances and boilers, and toys.

for Medicine Evaluation is resisting opening the approval process to public review, and the new agency was not functional on January 1, 1995 as planned. Once this is completed, and the initial regulations are issued, this will improve quickly.

The EU "New Approach Directives" are developed by a consensus of the regulatory system and the Council. The EU decided that the existing regulatory methods, like the U.S. FDA, were too expensive, restricted competition, and could not adjust to technical change. To fix these problems, the Council issued Council Resolution (85/C 136/01), which stated that a generic language approach and the use of third-party audits would result in protection of the health and safety of the public, reduce regulatory costs, and promote free movement of goods. To standardize the testing requirements, the Commission approved the *Certification and Technical Standards Directive* (89/181/EEC) as last amended by 94/10/EC, which required the use of harmonized standards.

While the technical directives may appear confusing, a standard format for them has evolved. The articles and Annex I are the mandatory requirements. The articles are written in EU legal jargon, but the annexes are intended to be technical documents that can be used to design, implement, and define the technical requirements. The methods are left to the choice of the manufacturers. The harmonized standards define the present state of the art.

Typical Technical Directives

Scope and Definitions

Article 1 defines the scope of the directive. Definitions of terms are given next. Regulatory compliance is basically meeting definitions. For example, in the *Machinery Directive,* "component" means that part of machinery the failure of which endangers the operator or personnel working with the machinery. If the case cracks and the operator is not exposed to danger, then the case is not a component.

Exemptions

This article defines what products are exempt. The list of products that are exempt may not be completely binding, and each exemption must be read with care. As an example, pharmaceutical products are covered by the *Medicinal Product Directive* (65/65/EEC), but if the pharmaceutical product is required to make a medical device function, then it is covered by the *Medical Device Directive.* As another example, machinery used on seagoing vessels is exempt from the *Machinery Directive*; however, any vessel under 500 tons is covered, as are the safety equipment used in hoists, fire safety equipment, and lifts used on boats. It cannot be assumed that particular equipment is not covered because its class of product is listed as an exemption; an authority should be consulted.

Free Movement Clause

This article requires the Member States to change their laws to permit the free movement of goods. There may be no restriction to the transfer of goods, including taxation. The Courts have been the major force in the free movement of goods. Citizens have been taking their Member States to court for restricting the free movement of goods.

Conformity Assessment Procedures

The following definitions are provided as an aid to understanding the conformity process.

Certification—Procedure in which a third party gives written assurance that a product, service, or process conforms to specific requirements.

Evaluation of Conformity—Systematic examination of the extent to which a product, process, or service fulfills specific requirements.

Harmonized Standard—Technical specification adopted by the Standing Committee of a directive whose compliance is obligatory.

Mandate—Formal designation of a standards organization to develop standards for the EU.

Mandatory Certification—Certification required by a regulation, directive, or decision that must be performed in order to place a product, service, or process on the market.

Notified Body—A government-sanctioned organization that has been designated as capable of evaluating a quality system or product to determine that it meets specific requirements. It is a registrar or a certified laboratory. For the EU, it must be published in the *Official Journal of the European Union.*

Transition Period—The time that elapses between the date a regulation or directive is passed until the Member States have transposed the requirements into national law. It is set in each legislation.

Reference Standards: Presumption of Conformity

The safety of products is ensured by the development of harmonized standards. For the standards to generate the necessary consumer confidence, it was essential that a flexible, mutual recognition system be established at the Community level for certification and the recognition of test results. "This has led to a...flexible and non-bureaucratic structure, in Europe, to be set up under the agent of the Commission within the existing European standardization infrastructure Comité Européen de Normalisation/Comité Européen de Normalisation Electrotechnique (CEN/CENELEC)."* CEN/CENELEC were authorized by the

---

* *The EU Modules for Conformity Assessment Directives,* St. Lucie Press, Boca Raton, FL, 1997.

Definition of Harmonized Standard

A technical specification that has been adopted by either CEN or CENELEC. It states the procedure for supplying information regarding technical standards and regulations. CEN and CENELEC, under their contract with the Commission, have defined the following kinds of harmonized standards:

A standards deal with fundamental concepts. EN 292 for machinery or EN 60601 for electro-medical equipment is an example of this category.

B standards deal with general safety aspects of a family of equipment. Examples are the safety clearance distance for a piece of machinery and a method of calculating safe forklift capacity. Examples for machinery are EN 294 and EN 563.

B2 standards deal with specific components or devices, such as the EN 60601 series on medical equipment or EN 115 for escalators and EN 281 for safety devices.

C standards are so-called "vertical" standards covering a single type of machine. An example is EN 670 for manure spreaders.

Commission to develop harmonized standards. A flexible certification and regulatory system was established through the EN 29000 and EN 45000 standards. There are also specific standards for individual product fields, such as the EN 46000 series for medical devices.

A designer would use the *A standards* to develop product specifications. In the design review section, application of the A standards must be documented, and these results are then included in the Technical Information File (TIF).* The *B and C standards* are the test methods and product testing which demonstrate that the product meets the requirements of the relevant directives.

*Presumption of Conformity***

According to the "New Approach Directives," if you conform to published, harmonized standards, you are presumed to be in compliance with the Direc-

---

* Also referred to as the Technical Construction File (TCF).
** Guide to the Implementation, EU-OP, 1993, p. 41.

Development of a Harmonized Standard

If at any of these steps the standard is rejected, the standard returns to the WG

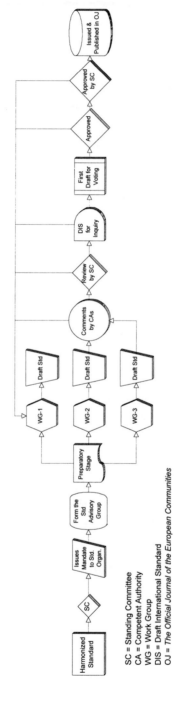

SC = Standing Committee
CA = Competent Authority
WG = Work Group
DIS = Draft International Standard
OJ = *The Official Journal of the European Communities*

tive. The standard must be published by the Commission in the *Official Journal of the European Communities*. The presumption of conformity depends on the following elements:

1. **Publication of the reference**—It must be published in the *Official Journal of the European Communities* in order to be used for the presumption of conformity. The main motive for publication by the Commission in the official journal is to set a clear date for all community members.

2. **Transposition**—The presumption of conformity is also dependent upon the transposition of the European standard into national standards. A standard does not confer presumption of conformity if it has not been transposed, even if the reference has been published in the *Official Journal of the European Communities*. On the other hand, it is not necessary for the transposition to take place in all Member States before it confers presumption of conformity. As long as at least one Member State has transposed it, the standard will confer presumption of conformity.*

Standing Committee

The Standing Committee acts as the agent of the Commission. There is a Standing Committee for each directive passed. The Standing Committee Article grants the committee the power to:

1. Implement the directive
2. Approve all harmonized and national standards and regulations
3. Authorize the Notified Bodies
4. Supervise the Community surveillance through a Directorate-General of the Commission
5. Be responsible for enacting the withdrawal of market authorization
6. Publish opinions on directives or suggestions for new directives

The Standing Committees are made up of two representatives from each Member State and a member from the Commission. The Commission member usually acts as chairman and cannot vote.

---

* Once a standard has been transposed by a Member State, compliance with the standard permits the free movement of goods throughout the EEA and the EU.

Safeguard Clause

The safeguard clause permits a Member State to withdraw a product from the market if the Competent Authority feels that the product represents a clear danger to the health and safety of its citizens. However, the Commission has placed very restrictive requirements on what can be removed from the market. The Member State must submit a report to the Commission outlining the reasons for its actions. The Commission will review the report, and the Member State cannot take any action until a decision is reached by the Commission.

Conformity Assessment Procedures

The EU has developed the *Modules of Conformity Assessment Directive* (93/465/EEC), which outlines a uniform procedure for conformity assessment. The individual annexes of each directive will designate which modules apply to the directive. A company, in conjunction with the Notified Body, selects the annexes which apply to its products. The individual modules are discussed in greater detail in Chapter 6.

Authorization to Place on the Market

These clauses define the requirements and responsibility for placing a product on the market. This article will specify that you must meet the essential requirements as stated in Annex I. (For further discussion of essential requirements, see Chapter 5.)

The definition of essential requirements states that an evaluation of the *intended purpose as defined in the TCF* must be made on the basis of the risks versus benefit analysis. This clause also states that *all* the relevant directives must be met. This is generally a straightforward process except for a totally new product. You can contact the Directorate-General that covers your product field for a preliminary evaluation before developing a new product.

Authorized Representative

A person must be designated as your official representative when placing a product on the market. This agent acts on your behalf when dealing with Competent Authorities, Commission Directorates-General, Notified Bodies, and Standing Committees. The agent is usually the importer, who also makes sure that the proper labeling and documentation accompany the product to its des-

---

Essential Requirements

The latest definition of essential requirements is from 95/C 172/02: "Any apparatus, appliance, component, device, equipment, machinery, or service offered for sale in the EU must be designed and manufactured in such a way that, when used under the conditions and for the purposes intended, they will not compromise, directly or indirectly, the clinical condition or the safety of the patients, the safety and health of users and, where applicable, other persons, and the safety of property. Any risks, which may be associated with their use, must be acceptable when weighed against the benefits to the patient or customer and are compatible with a high level of protection of health and safety requirements lists in the relevant directives."

---

tination. You cannot replace this person without proper notification under the directive surveillance requirements. The authorized representative is similar to a power of attorney in the United States.

Surveillance

Many of the directives, such as the *Medical Device Directive, Machinery Directive, Human Medicinal Products Directive,* etc., have formal surveillance. All customer complaints and field problems have to be documented and reviewed by management. The procedure should be in the TCF. For risky products or an ISO 9000 quality management system, when used to meet the essential requirements, a formal reporting program to the appropriate Directorate-General will be required.

Notified Bodies

The idea underlying the "New Approach Directives" is to limit direct involvement by government. The EU only wants governmental bodies to intervene when it is absolutely necessary to ensure compliance with the essential requirements.* This principle is fully consistent with the fact that the authorities are still required to be responsible for surveillance of the market and the use of the

---

* This is made clear in the general clause concerning placing on the market, which appears in all the directives.

products. The EU developed the Notified Bodies to perform the auditing and market surveillance. The Notified Body is appointed by the Member State for specific directives, and product or service approval must come from an official Notified Body for the directives which apply. For example, a Notified Body for the *Toy Safety Directive* cannot authorize a tractor.

The various modules provide for the involvement of bodies at different levels (type-examination, product surveillance, approval of quality assurance, and verification). The purpose of the directives is to define the general criteria which these bodies must satisfy in order to be deemed competent. It is the task of each Member State to designate them and to notify the Commission and the other Member States. The Notified Bodies must demonstrate that they satisfy the criteria laid down in the European standards (EN 45000 series). For example, the fact that they are accredited means that they are presumed to comply with the criteria laid down in the directives.*

The EU Notified Body approval process makes it possible to distinguish between the act of designation and the act of certifying compliance. Since the Notified Body is appointed by a Member State and approved by the Commission, the actions and findings of a Notified Body are a legally binding act. The Notified Body can be an independent organization, part of a Competent Authority, or a national laboratory.

CE Marking

The CE Marking is the legal symbol that a product is in compliance with the relevant directives at the time the product is sold. Outdated products cannot be

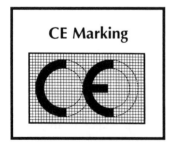

stockpiled in the EU to be sold. The CE Marking is affixed to let the Custom Union and Competent Authorities know that the product is in compliance. This can create some confusion because of the different transition periods of the directives. It must be permanently affixed to the outside of the product. There are a few cases in which it can be placed on the product packaging rather than on the product. These few instances are stated in the directives. Usually they are for medical devices. The CE Marking must follow the proportions in the box and cannot be smaller than five millimeters.

---

* OJ No. C 267, 1989, p. 3.

Wrongly Affixing the CE Marking

This article grants the EU all the necessary power needed to withdraw a product from the market. It enables the EU to refuse entry, remove a product from the market, issue fines, and even impose a prison sentence for not conforming to the EU Directives. This article also grants the EU immunity from liability in the event of a mistake.

Appeal of a Decision

This establishes the appeal process. The first appeal is to the Standing Committee, and the process takes at least six months. During the entire appeal process, **your product cannot be marketed**. If you are turned down by the Standing Committee, you may appeal to the Court of First Instance. Court of First Instance appeals are handled by the Court of Justice.

Confidentiality

This article makes confidentiality a legal and binding requirement of both parties. The Competent Authority, Notified Body, and Standing Committee can be found criminally liable for failure to comply. **All product or service information supplied to EU governmental bodies is confidential and does not have to be shared with the customer.** The EU courts have taken a strong stance on breach of confidentiality. They do not believe there is any reason to share information with anyone but a governmental body that has a need to know the information.

Annex I: Essential Requirements

This annex defines the essential requirements that a product must meet to be placed on the market. The essential requirements are the processes required to protect the health and safety of EU citizens and the environment. (For further discussion, see Chapter 10.) This is a technical document that defines what must be done, but does not define the "how to." The answer to each point in the annex should be in the TCF even if the answer is "It does not apply because…" It you choose not to follow the harmonized standards, you must prove that your product still conforms to the essential requirements. No matter what conformity assessment procedure you choose to follow, you will have to meet the essential requirements.

Conclusion

All of these articles and annexes form the EU Directive. All technical "New Approach Directives" follow this format. There are other formats for non-technical fields, but the information is the same. The directive will usually include at least these provisions, but there may be other articles and annexes as well. The directives are the enforceable laws of the EU. If you market a product or service in the EU, you must comply with the appropriate directives. If you do not, you can be fined and your product can be withdrawn from the market. **If your product does not comply and it injures an EU or EEA citizen, whoever is designated as the manufacturer can go to prison.** The regulatory process is not yet fully functional, but it will be within the next two years. Products are already being withdrawn from the market and fines are being imposed. For further discussion of the benefits and liability of the EU, see Section II.

Section II

Why?

A discussion of the benefits
and liability of EU compliance

4

Benefits and Liability

Complying with the EU Directives opens the largest single market in the world. The European Union accounts for 40% of the world's gross national product and over one-fifth of the total global trade in goods—more than either the United States or Japan.* Including its associate members and harmonization agreements, over 70 countries worldwide, including the United States and Japan, have adopted at least some of the EU Directives. Maintaining your "global edge" will depend upon your understanding of the EU Directives.

The European Union has 15 members and the European Economic Area (EEA) has another 4 members. The EEA plays an active role in the EU. It adopts all of the EU Directives and is actively involved in the writing of standards for the EU. If you comply with the EU Directives, you can also market your product within the EEA. The EU considers the EEA a transition group. It is expected that all of these countries will become full Member States in the future.

The Members of the EEA

Swiss Confederacy
Iceland
Norway
Principality of Liechtenstein

The EU also has several associate members. An associate member will adopt at least some of the directives. The associate members of the EU include Greenland, Turkey, Cyprus, Malta, several of the former Soviet Union countries, almost all of the Mediterranean countries, and 70 countries in Africa, the Pacific, and the Caribbean. Associate countries are not required to pay tariffs

---

* These figures are from *The European Union and World Trade,* published by the Office for Official Publications of the European Communities, June 1995, p. 5.

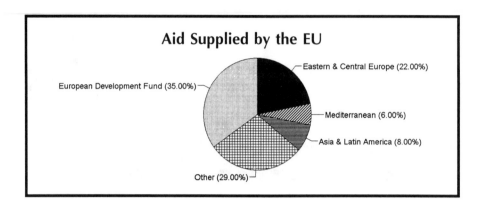

and receive a great deal of economic aid from the EU. It is expected that most of the associate members will eventually join the EU when they meet the required levels of economic independence. Cyprus, Turkey, and Malta have already applied for membership.

On June 22, 1993, the Copenhagen European Council adopted a provision which states that the former Soviet and Eastern bloc countries will be able to join the EU as soon as the required political and economic levels are reached. The EU provides aid to assist these countries in reaching this goal. In the future, all of these markets will be open to manufacturing and service industries that comply with the EU Directives.

Many of these countries already require the CE Marking to sell products within their borders. *The CE Marking opens doors.* It enables you to expand your available markets with *one* compliance process rather than several. With the CE Marking, you can market your product anywhere within the EU and the EEA, as well as many of the EU associate countries.

The CE Marking must follow these proportions:

Not only are the Member States and associate countries available to you, but the EU has also signed many agreements with individual countries which make a specific directive law in that country. A good example of this is the new *Good Clinical Practices* (*GCP*), which will be released some time in 1997.* The *GCP* was written by the International Conference on Harmoni-

---

* The official draft version of the new *GCP* is available now from St. Lucie Press.

zation (ICH). All members of the ICH have agreed to make the new *GCP* law in their countries. The three major members of the ICH are the EU, Japan, and the United States. The *GCP* will go into effect in the EU on July 1, 1997, and it is on the fast track in both the United States and Japan and will probably be passed in the fourth quarter of 1997. The new *GCP* will allow a clinical test to be used to show compliance in all members countries of the ICH without retesting. Sixty-two percent of the cost of developing a new drug is the cost of testing; the new *GCP* is expected to lower this cost.

The CE Marking is considered a symbol of quality in Europe. The lowest bidder does not always get the contract in Europe. Europeans believe in buying a good quality product that will last, even if the price is higher. The CE Marking is perceived as ensuring this quality.

In addition to the large number of markets that become open to you with compliance to the EU Directives, compliance can lower your overall business costs. The emphasis on documentation in the EU is often perceived as increasing the costs of business. However, from the experience of those who have complied, overall product documentation tends to decrease. by 10 to 20%. The quality system (usually ISO 9000) required for EU compliance ensures that you evaluate your company documents and determine their uses. Often a company discovers that it is generating many documents that are redundant, not used, and unnecessary. Compliance also reduces the number of documents required

---

DuPont Benefits from Compliance

DuPont's Columbia, Maryland facility had over 5,000 test methods that had to be reviewed and updated over four years. When the facility implemented its ISO 9001 quality system, it eliminated over 40% of its test methods. There were 27 different methods for determining the pH of a solution; just one was substituted. The facility also instituted a calibration procedure which ensured that the results were correct. There was no consistent calibration procedure prior to this. Thirty-five percent of the facility's sampling and te ting was retesting and was unnecessary. Procedures were developed which set the criteria for when a retest was necessary. Retesting was cut by 90%. Testing costs were reduced by $2.5 million per year. In addition, the workload of individual employees was reduced, allowing them the time to concentrate on the true problems. This had the additional effect of greatly increasing morale and reducing customer complaints by 75%.

because one set is used for the EU and the EEA rather than one for each individual country.

As you are evaluating these documents, it is logical to evaluate the processes that generate them. Many companies perform testing that is redundant or unnecessary. However, because these processes have not been reviewed, the redundancy is not discovered until the company builds its EU quality system.

Another benefit is the documented procedures. You may have just as many emergencies documented in your new quality system, but they are less stressful if you have a documented procedure for addressing them.

The third-party audit, necessary for EU compliance, gives you a quantitative measurement of the resources, manpower, and equipment necessary to implement your business plan. Because you have documented your business process, you will know what is required to perform each business function. This often will reveal the "bottlenecks" which limit your production rate. It is very difficult to plan where you are going if you do not know where you are now.

ACME Electrical Motor Division

ACME decided to combine two of its plants that produced electrical motors. One plant was relatively new and the other was much older. The older plant hired a new plant manager who decided to implement ISO 9000. The older plant had experienced numerous quality and delivery problems. Its scrap rate on a particular motor was as high as 25%.

The new plant manager decided that the best way to fix the quality problems was to implement ISO 9001. ACME needed to choose a registered quality system because many of its products were being exported to the EU. During the implementation process, the company identified problem areas and was able to correct them. After becoming registered to ISO 9001, the scrap rate dropped to less than 1%. The on-time delivery rate was greater than 98%. Employee morale and training improved. Overall productivity was greatly enhanced. The company also increased its business by 20%, because it was in compliance with the EU Directives.

The parent management had originally planned to close the older plant; however, after the improvements from implementing ISO 9001, the new plant was closed and operations were moved to the older plant. The company increased local employment by 360 jobs.

While not all components are covered by directives, in many cases buying components which do comply simplifies your compliance process. If you buy a product or component that is in compliance, you do not have to retest it to ensure compliance for your system. You only have to test those areas that are not yet in compliance. If you make components, you can increase your customer base by complying with the EU Directives. **Many EU companies are demanding that their non-EU suppliers become in compliance with the EU Directives.**

Compliance with the EU Directives is also simpler than the U.S. system. Rather than writing laws which state the specifics of every product, the EU Directives are generic in nature. They are written so that they do not need to be updated every time there is a technological advance. A manufacturer is presumed to be in compliance with the directive if he can prove compliance to the harmonized standards that apply.

Even if you do not export to Europe, you will probably still have to comply in the near future in order to compete in the international market. Probably one-third of all countries will adopt the EU Directives, and most likely all non-agricultural products will have to meet the EU Directives by the year 2000. It is already the largest single compliance method available and will only continue to grow. In many areas in the United States, the laws are already harmonized with the EU Directives.

Deciding not to comply simply because you don't want to do it or because you don't believe it will affect your business does not make sense. The "management-by-denial approach" will not enable you to maintain your international competitiveness. The U.S. steel industry is a prime example. It failed to comply on an international level and to keep up with industry trends. As a result, the Japanese and Korean steel industries took the Americans' business. If history teaches us one thing it is that the better economic process always wins. Not making a decision *is* a decision. Once you lose your market share, it is extremely difficult to get it back.

The liability laws in the EU are more stringent than in the United States. The penalties are higher, but this is compensated for by greater liability protection. If you are in compliance with all relevant directives, you cannot be penalized if your product injures an EU citizen, even if the directive or standard is found to be wrong at a later date. For example, under EU law, you cannot be sued for liability damages for breast implants (see Appendix 2 for the *EU Liability Directive*) if the implants met current EU law for health and safety. However, if you are not in compliance with all relevant directives and standards, you are criminally as well as financially liable. You can be fined, your product can be withdrawn from the market, or the manufacturer can be imprisoned. **Under EU law, a specific person must be named as the manufacturer and that person is personally liable for damages caused by his or her products.** You are guilty until proven innocent under the EU judicial system. If your product is withdrawn from the market for non-compliance, it may not be placed back on the market until you prove that it is in full compliance. This process takes a minimum of six months and usually longer. In that time, you will have lost the confidence of the consumer, even if you prove that your product is in compliance. While in the past the chance of being sued was lower in the EU, it is now just as high as in the United States.

Another twist to the EU Directives is in the advertising of a product. The advertising of a product or service is considered a contract between the business and the consumer. If you state that your process will make the consumer a millionaire in a week, the consumer better have a million dollars within seven days. If not, you are personally liable and can be sued for that million dollars.

In the EU, the state pays all medical bills of its citizens, so the state has a vested interest in decreasing medical costs. This is why health and safety are emphasized as one of the pillars of the EU. Liability laws are written to reflect this. The state will not be sympathetic to your position if it costs it a great deal of money.

One of the main purposes of the third-party compliance system is to transfer the cost of compliance to the business. The state is not responsible for paying an auditor to ensure your system meets the directives and standards. You, as the manufacturer or service provider, must pay the Notified Body to audit your system. While this cost can be significant, the overall costs and time are usually much lower under the EU system. The overall costs of compliance have dropped by 50% under the EU system. This is particularly beneficial to small manufacturers.

Drop in Approval Time

Manufacturers of active implantable medical devices have found that the approval time has dropped from a minimum of two years to only six months in the EU. The savings to this industry have been astronomical. You can be generating income from your product in the EU while it is still sitting on some bureaucrat's desk in the United States.

The benefits of the EU compliance system far outweigh the detriments. By reading the EU Directives, and understanding their intentions, you can avoid the "pitfalls" and increase your international market share. **Whatever happens on the political and social front,**

the single-market economy *will* **go forward**. It is important not to confuse cultural differences with economic interests. The market is too new for the individual citizens to see many benefits yet. However, business is already enjoying the benefits under the EU system, and eventually this will translate into increased jobs and wages. As these benefits are realized, support for the EU will grow within its own boundaries.

Section III

How?

**A brief overview of
obtaining compliance to
the EU Directives and standards**

5

Regulated Products and Regulatory Symbols

The EU approach to certification is founded upon the *Certification and Technical Standards Directive* (83/189/EEC), as last amended by 94/10/EC, *Good Laboratory Practices (GLP)*, and the *Modules of Conformity Assessment* (93/465/EEC). Under these directives, only products or services that pose a risk to health, safety, and the environment are regulated products. If food is excluded,

---

Regulated Products Under "New Approach Directives"

87/404/EEC	Simple pressure vessels
88/378/EEC	Safety of toys
89/106/EEC	Construction products
89/336/EEC	Electromagnetic compatibility
89/392/EEC	Machinery
89/686/EEC	Personal protective equipment
90/384/EEC	Non-automatic weighing machines
90/385/EEC	Active, implantable, medical devices
90/396/EEC	Appliances burning gaseous fuels
91/263/EEC	Telecommunications terminal equipment
92/42/EEC	New hot-water boilers fired with liquid or gaseous fuels
94/09/EC	Equipment used in potentially explosive atmospheres

---

probably 90% of all products shipped to Europe are regulated. Regulated products are primarily industrial and commercial products. Products for personal or home use that are not electrically powered or provide transportation are usually not regulated in the EU. They are regulated by the individual Member States. Since the largest category of exported products to the EU is electrically powered products, most exporters will be required to follow the EU Directives and become involved with Notified Bodies.

The first step on the road to compliance with the EU Directives is to determine if your product is regulated. The box at the bottom of the previous page lists the areas for which "New Approach Directives" have been written. These are all regulated products. If your product fits in one of these categories, you will need the CE Marking. If your product does not fit in one of these categories, it may be regulated under the "old approach directives." Medicinal products, instruments, and automobiles are covered by "old approach directives."

After determining if your product is regulated, you need to do a risks assessment in order to classify which modules of conformity assessment apply. The classification of your product or service is in the relevant directives. The risks assessment requirements are found in Annex I, Essential Requirements, in most directives. Since most safety hazards are the result of the design of the

Safeguard Clause and the EOTC

The *GLP, Modules of Conformity Assessment,* and the harmonized standards address some of the concerns of citizens about the safety of products placed on the market. These directives and standards allow the Member States to restrict the free movement of goods through the Safeguard Clause. These issues have been addressed by the Commission in a series of opinions that narrowly define what can be restricted by the Safeguard Clause. It can only be used when there is a clearly documented danger. The Member States must submit a report to the Commission for review and approval whenever they enact the Safeguard Clause. Until approval is given, the product cannot be pulled from the market.

The European Organization on Testing and Certification (EOTC) was formed to deal with conformity assessment issues. It has developed standards for accrediting the Notified Bodies to ensure mutual recognition of test results by the Member States. Furthermore, the EOTC encouraged the development of the CB Scheme for electrical testing and MOUs between Notified Bodies and testing organizations outside the EU. The EOTC also develops guidelines for testing in various directives.

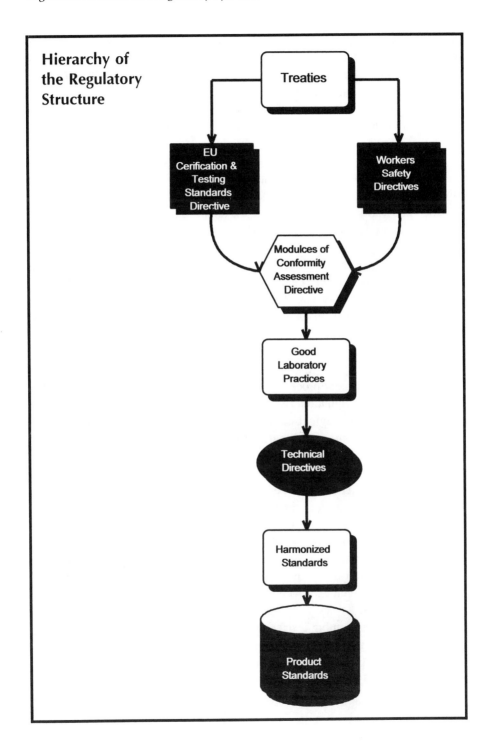

Hierarchy of the Regulatory Structure

Treaties

EU Cerification & Testing Standards Directive

Workers Safety Directives

Modulces of Conformity Assessment Directive

Good Laboratory Practices

Technical Directives

Harmonized Standards

Product Standards

product, risks assessment is considered to be the primary method for ensuring that the safety aspects are adequately addressed. Furthermore, the intention of the *Certification and Technical Standards Directive* (83/189/EEC), *GLP,* and *Modules of Conformity Assessment Directive* is to build public trust in the conformity assessment process. The public is more likely to accept a system if people know that risks assessment will be done for products placed on the market.

The EU Directives will probably not use the term risks assessment, but they will tell you that you must evaluate the hazards of a product. The Notified Body will check to see if you have done a formal risks assessment, and you will fail the conformity assessment if it is not done. Many things in the EU Directives are open to interpretation. The EU assumes that when reading the directives, you will be an active reader and interpret their meaning. The Notified Body will interpret the directives. If you have questions regarding the various implications in a directive, check with a competent consultant or a Notified Body. Another way to ensure that you understand the meaning of a directive is to read the Commission Opinion on the directive. The Commission is now required to issue an Opinion with each new directive.

Risks assessment is a formal analysis that determines the potential hazards to which the user may be exposed and the likelihood that the hazard will occur. The EU risks assessment process is outlined in the *Risks Assessment Directive* (93/67/EEC) and Regulation (EC) 793/93, both of which will probably be revised soon. As the original directive is written, it appears to apply only to chemicals and environmental hazards. However, it actually applies to all regulated products. The new directive will clarify this. The Technical Construction File (TCF) for all regulated products must contain a formal risks assessment.

The technical directives can be confusing when discussing risks assessment because the guidelines are written generically. This was done deliberately to eliminate the problems associated with rapid changes in technology. The detailed technical requirements are spelled out in the harmonized "A standard" published in the *Official Journal of the European Communities.* To understand what is required, you must have a copy of all the official documents that deal with a particular directive. If you are missing a piece, you cannot finish interpreting the puzzle.

The trick in performing a risks assessment is to convert the general statements in the essential requirements into a list of questions that directly apply to your product. The answer to the questions will clarify what needs to be done, what the potential risks are, and the likelihood that the risk will occur. Each

Risks Assessment: *PEA,* Annex I

1.0   General requirements

1.0.1 Principles of integrated explosion safety

Equipment and protective systems intended for use in potentially explosive atmospheres must be designed from the point of view of integrated explosion safety.

In this connection, the manufacturer must take measures:

- above all, if possible, to prevent the formation of explosive atmospheres which may be produced or released by equipment and by protective systems themselves.

- to prevent the ignition of explosive atmospheres, taking into account the nature of every electrical and non-electrical source of ignition.

- should an explosion nevertheless occur which could directly or indirectly endanger persons and, as the case may be, domestic animals or property, to halt it immediately and/or to limit the range of explosion flames and explosion pressures to a sufficient level of safety.

1.0.2 Equipment and protective systems must be designed and manufactured after due analysis of possible operating faults in order as far as possible to preclude dangerous situations.

Any misuse which can reasonably be anticipated must be taken into account.

In order to meet these requirements, you must do a formal risks assessment. Notice that the wording does not say "risks assessment," but it is one of the things that the Notified Body will be checking for when doing your conformity assessment.

statement in Annex I must be addressed, even if you think that it does not apply to your product. If the hazard is not likely to occur, then you do not have to address it, but you should explain in the TCF why you think it will not occur. If a hazard is life threatening, it must be addressed. Each statement can generate one or more questions, and the individual questions should lead to a clear answer. The following page provides examples of forming checklists of questions upon which your risks assessment will be based for the *Low Voltage Directive.*

The essential requirements can be subdivided into two types of hazards: those that reside in equipment, such as electrical power, and those that arise

Forming a Checklist from the *LVD*

2. Protection against hazards arising from the electrical equipment*

   Measures of a technical nature should be prescribed in accordance with *point 1*, in order to ensure:

   a) that persons and domestic animals are adequately protected against danger of physical injury or other harm which might be caused by electrical contact direct or indirect;

   b) that temperatures, arcs or radiation which would cause a danger are not produced;

   c) that persons, domestic animals and property are adequately protected against non-electrical dangers caused by the electrical equipment which are revealed by experience;

   d) that the insulation must be suitable for foreseeable conditions.

   ---

   *Excerpted from the *Low Voltage Directive,* Annex I.

Generating a Checklist for the *LVD*

2a. What are the electrical dangers?

   How can I prevent exposure to live voltage?

   What must happen in order for exposure to live voltage to occur?

   How likely is that to occur?

2b. At what temperature will this equipment operate?

   Are there any "hot spots"?

   How do I prevent "hot spots"?

2c. If used as intended, are there any non-electrical dangers caused by the equipment?

   How likely are they to occur?

   How do I prevent them?

2d. What are the foreseeable conditions against which the insulation must provide protection?

   What is the likely exposure and the duration?

from outside equipment, such as a short in a power cord or a broken case. The official list of standards indicates the technical documents that state the present state of the art and what an acceptable solution is. The "A standards" outline the dangers and the methods for addressing or preventing them. Either the product standard or the "A standard" will list standards that can be adopted to determine the compliance of your equipment. A testing laboratory or a compliance specialists can help sort through the design trade-offs.

Most magazine articles dealing with EU compliance have focused on the CE Marking. All "New Approach Directives" require CE Marking certification. However, there are other certification markings which are also required. For example, the EU Commission has converted the national *LVD* marks into EU-wide marks. Several of the "old approach directives" are for regulated products, but they do not require the CE Marking. Examples are medicinal products and instruments. Eventually, all regulated products will be covered by "New Approach Directives" and will require the CE Marking. This is a very limited number of products. Some portion of these products usually fall under at least one "New Approach Directive" and require the CE Marking. For example, if a medicinal product is delivered by a medical device, it will require the CE Marking.

A variety of compliance symbols are used in the EU to indicate compliance. The main symbol is the CE Marking. It represents compliance to *all* the rel-

CE Marking

evant standards and "New Approach Directives." With this symbol, a product or service can be freely marketed throughout the EU. The box to the left shows the required proportions of the CE Marking. It can be expanded or contracted, as long as the proportions are maintained. However, the CE Marking is not the only symbol that you may have to apply to your product.

Most commercial and industrial equipment falls under either the *Machinery Directive* or the *Equipment Used in Potentially Explosive Atmospheres Directive*, depending upon whether the primary hazard is electrical or mechanical.

ECO-Label

Household appliances such as refrigerators and blenders are also regulated products. They are covered by the *LVD* and by the *Appliance Directives*. The *Appliance Directives* focus on the reduction of energy use and recycling. The ECO-Label is required for household appliances. It indicates that the product is environmentally friendly. ISO 14000 Environmental Management System registration is not required for the ECO-Label, but the Parliament is leaning in that direction. The directives and standards are designed to encourage consumers to buy

Recycling Symbol

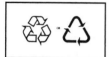

energy-efficient appliances and to recycle their old ones. The Recycling Symbol is required on any product that can be recycled. By international agreement, the Recycling Symbol is used on most plastic products. It is also found on most plastic products molded in the United States. Household appliances and cars are required to be recycled in the EU and this symbol will appear on them.

The Percent Recycle Symbol is used to indicate to the consumer the percentage of recycled material in a product. Most paper and plastic products will

% Recycle

have this symbol. National laws cover the requirements for the use of the Recycling Symbol. German laws are quite strict, and the EU Plastic Waste Proposal is patterned after them. The recycling issue should be addressed in the TCF. Also, the ECO-Label requires that any disposable products, shipped in reasonable volumes,* must have a formal recycling program.

In addition to the ECO-Label, electrical household appliances must have an Energy Label. The Energy Label is used in conjunction with the CE Marking to symbolize that a product is in compliance with the *Appliance Directives*. There our two energy labels, the Oven Label and the Energy Label. The Energy Label is used to indicate annual energy consumption. The Oven Label shows the energy used by the oven at different settings. Both labels must appear on ovens.

Energy Label

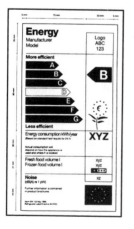

Oven Label

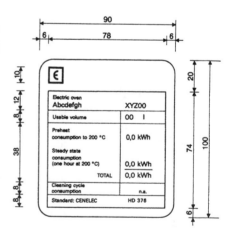

---

* Under EU law, "reasonable volume" is a legal term which defines a set amount of waste. This amount is set in the directives and depends upon the product.

Energy Star

Gas appliances and hot-water heaters also require labels. The CE Marking is required for Directive 90/396/EEC and 92/42/EEC. The ECO-Label and the Energy Label can also be used. If you manufacture gas appliances, you must become ISO 9001/2 registered. Hot-water tanks and boilers must also have the Energy Star as well as the CE Marking. Gas appliances must use EC-Type Verification, and the Notified Body's identification symbol appears under the Energy Star. Commercial and industrial equipment which perform functions like household appliances should have the Energy Label. The information that appears on the Energy Label must appear in the instruction manual as well.

The Reusable Package symbol is placed on packaging that can be recycled. It is designed to encourage the reduction and recycling of packaging. Most

Reusable Package

manufactures of large appliances, such as washers, must use reusable packaging. The seller is to pick up the shipping container and return it to the manufacturer.

The Europeans have put a great deal of emphasis on recycling and reusing. Most manufacturers that ship to the EU will need to have a formal recycling plan. The symbols discussed above and the laws regarding packaging and recycling are in the *EU Packaging Waste* and *ECO-Label Directives*. Their numbers are Directive 93/C 205/01, Regulation (EEC) No. 880/92, Commission Decision 93/326/EEC, and Commission Decision 93/517/EEC. While recycling is still under national authority, proposal 93/C 205/01 is patterned after German law. The ECO-Label requires a formal recycling program.

Another common authorization symbol that may have to be placed with the CE Marking is the PEA Label. This symbol is used to signify compliance with

PEA Label

the *Equipment Used in Potentially Explosive Atmospheres Directive*. It is placed on equipment that may be used in atmospheres which may explode if the machine fails. Along with the PEA Label, there will be a symbol which indicates the type of explosive atmosphere. The three types of atmospheres identified in the directive are gas, dust, and pressure. Each of these has a symbol. There are many other symbols that you may have to place on your product, depending upon the requirements of the relevant directives. "N' is also used by the *Pressure Vessel Directive* (87/404/EEC) to indicate compliance. The Notified Body's identification number appears under the symbol.

Gas Label	Pressure Label	Dust Label

Telecommunication equipment must have the CE Marking plus one of the additional marks attached to the Public Telecommunication Net (PTN). In addition to traditional equipment such as faxes, many business machines and other pieces of equipment will need these symbols to attach to the PTN. To

---

Telecommunications Symbols

ANNEX VI*
Marking for Terminal Equipment Referred to in Article 11(1)

The CE Conformity Marking shall consist of the initial "CE" taking the following form, following by the additional information referred to in Article 11 (1):

CE Marking	Identification Number of the Notified Body	Symbol of Suitability for Connection to the Public Telecommunication Network (Chi)

See the *Official Journal of the European Communities* for character font.
- If the CE Marking is reduced or enlarged, the proportions given in the above drawings must be respected.
- The various components of the CE Marking must have substantially the same vertical dimension, which may not be less than 5 mm.**
- The identification number for the Notified Body is considered a symbol.

---

  * Excerpted from the *Telecommunications Directive* (91/263/EEC).
** Text inserted and illustrations in Annex VI revised per Article 11 (12) of Directive 93/68/EEC (p. 19).

prevent restriction of the computer industry, the Commission has issued the Notchi Symbol to indicate that the product can be attached to a LAN but not to the PTN. Since some the directives have not been passed yet, it is not clear how the LAN products will be handled.

Foods and food products are not covered by the "New Approach Directives"; however, food processing and packaging equipment is covered. Furthermore, food additives, colorants, and plastic additives are covered. They require the CE Marking. The Food Symbol is used on any product that comes in contact with food to indicate compliance with the food additive and material directives. Materials and additives cannot interact with food such that they leave residue that would increase health risks. These additives and materials are regulated for the most part by the European Medicine Evaluation Agency (EMEA); however, there is a Standing Committee for the *Food Additive Directive* that is separate from the EMEA.

Food Symbol

Telecommunications Symbols

ANNEX VII
Marking for Equipment Referred to in Article 11 (4)*

Notchi

- If the marking is reduced or enlarged, the proportions given in the graduated drawing to the left must be respected.
- The various components of the CE Marking must have substantially the same vertical dimension, which may not be less than 5 mm.
- This marking is for equipment that is not hooked up to the PTN, but can be hooked to a LAN. It indicates that your equipment is *not* in compliance with the directives. However, you must go through a Notified Body to place it on your equipment.**

---

* Mark displayed in Annex VII revised per Article 11 (13) of Directive 93/68/EEC (p. 19).

** Yes, we know this is ridiculous, but even in Europe regulatory officials sometimes get overzealous.

Official Abbreviations of the Member States

	Abbreviation
Austria	AT
Belgium	BL
Germany	DE
Denmark	DK
Greece	EL
Spain	ES
Finland	FS
France	FR
United Kingdom	UK
Ireland	IE
Italy	IT
Portugal	PT
Sweden	SE
Luxembourg	L
Netherlands	NL

The symbol for ECC Pattern Approval for instruments is the abbreviation in the designated font. The identification number of the Notified Body should be placed under the abbreviation.

Instrumentation also has separate compliance symbols. They only apply to instruments that are used to determine amounts for commercial purposes, such as balances and scales. The symbol is the official abbreviation of the Member State where the manufacturer first applied for approval. The directive states the proper font. This is called ECC Pattern Type Approval. The approval process is very similar to Module F and Module G, except it predates the ISO 9000 quality standards. ISO used this system as a pattern for its quality system (ISO 9000).

There are other compliance symbols, depending upon your product. Some products will require the other symbols in addition to the CE Marking. We have reviewed the most common symbols that you will encounter. The key to unlocking the puzzle of EU compliance is reading the relevant directives.

6

Modules of Conformity Assessment

The *Modules of Conformity Assessment Directive* (93/465/EEC) provides a uniform protocol for assessing the safety of a product or service. Using a generic approach, like the ISO 9000 quality standards, the directive can be applied to any type of product or service. This modular approach simplifies the regulatory process by providing a consistent format across the EU. This directive is the cornerstone of the free movement of goods and forces the Member States to stop using testing specifications to erect barriers to trade.

There are eight modules. Which module you choose depends not only on the type of product or service, but also on the degree of risk to health, safety, and the environment. The modules do not become mandatory until they are selected. The manufacturer or service provider usually works with the Notified Body to choose the appropriate modules. In most cases, more than one module is necessary. The next few chapters will examine the implementation of the individual modules in greater depth.

The EU Modular Approach to Conformity Assessment focuses on two concepts. The first concept is standardized testing to verify compliance of a product or service. The second is that a manufacturer or service provider must have a quality management system. The purpose of this system is to provide the quality assurance that the product was assembled properly, compliance was verified, and non-conformities were corrected. The differences between the new approach and the old one are the emphasis on inputs and the use of a uniform third-party audit system to check that the compliance system is operating. This has been done in the United States for medicines, medical devices,

---

Modules of Conformity Assessment

Module A is the simplest. A manufacturer or service provider self-declares to be in compliance and prepares a Technical Information File (TIF).

Module B applies to products that have to meet technical standards. Generally, a Notified Body must perform the EC Type-Examination. Module B is always used in conjunction with another module.

Module C is conformity to type. The EC Type-Examination is carried out by a Notified Body. The manufacturer prepares a TIF and issues a Declaration of Conformity.

Module D covers production of products with some degree of risk. The supplier must be registered to ISO 9002 and the EC Type-Examination must be performed by a Notified Body.

Module E covers production of products with a lesser degree of risk. It is aimed at distributors and contract assemblers. They must register to ISO 9003.

---

toys, etc., but has never been applied uniformly to all products. Furthermore, even in industries where outside surveillance is required, lack of funds has produced uneven results. In the medical field, there are companies that have been producing products for many years and have never had an FDA inspection. As the material manager of Fisher Price, I worked with a company that molded medical products for over 30 years. This company makes medical disposables but has never had an on-site FDA inspection. The company is now trying to upgrade its facility to meet the EU requirements and is having difficulty getting into compliance. The company's lack of experience with audits is severely handicapping its efforts.

Under the EU system, the funding problem has been eliminated with two approaches. The individual company, not the government, is responsible for paying for the audit. This ensures that everyone has periodic audits to guarantee they are in compliance. The company is also responsible for paying for any testing necessary to certify a product. These two approaches eliminate the barriers to the free movement of goods caused by budget differences between the Member States. The Notified Body can either be a testing lab or a quality registrar. Even if they have the same name, such as BSI, the testing lab and quality registrar are different organizations. The Notified Body is appointed and certified by the Competent Authority of each Member State. The Competent Authority then submits the Notified Body to the Commission. After ap-

Notified Bodies and Sales

Just like Americans, Europeans often trust certain product names more than others. This can carry over to Notified Bodies. For example, Europeans feel that pharmaceutical products are better made by Americans and the Swiss. If two similar bottles of aspirin were on the shelf, Europeans would be more likely to buy an American product with a Swiss Notified Body than an English one.

Another example is machinery. A German Notified Body will give your product greater consumer confidence than an Italian one. Many consumers equate German machinery with quality.

proval by the Commission, the Notified Body becomes a government-sanctioned body. This makes its decisions and actions legally binding. **Your Notified Body must be certified to the particular directive under which your product or service falls. It is important that you are certified by the *correct* Notified Body.** If you choose the wrong one, your CE Marking is worthless. Your product can be pulled from the market, you can be fined, and in some cases, you can go to prison. The best way to ensure that you choose the correct Notified Body is to read the directives. You should also consult your customers. Customers will often have a preference for a Notified Body. Even though Notified Bodies are equal under the law, your customers may feel that one is superior to another. The identification symbol of the Notified Body appears next to the CE Marking and, therefore, will probably affect sales. You should also verify your choice by either calling the European Union or reading the decision of the directive to ensure that that Notified Body is listed for your product or service.

The Notified Body must be located in Europe. Even though there are Notified Bodies with U.S. offices, the actual Certificates of Conformity are issued by the EU office. Because the U.S. government has not yet set up a government organization to approve Notified Bodies, these branch offices are private companies in the United States. Their actions are not legally binding, as they are in the EU. Until the U.S. government responds appropriately, there can be no U.S. Notified Bodies.

There are three ways to accomplish testing outside the EU and not have to retest within the EU. First, testing can be done outside the EU under the Competent Body (CB) Scheme. The CB Scheme, run by the International Electrotechnical Commission (IEC), allows testing to be accepted among members. It covers most electrical products and components. Testing can be performed in the United States and will not have to be redone in the EU. There are over 50

What Is the CB Scheme?

The CB Scheme is a laboratory accredited by the IEC to award a CB Test Certificate to a manufacturer for a product. Each National Member of the CB Scheme pledges to recognize the others' test results. The CB Test Certificate means that the results can be used to gain product approval in any member country without retesting. The United States joined the CB Scheme in 1992.

members to the CB Scheme. The tests must be performed according to each member's published specifications. The specifications are published in the *CB Bulletin*. In the United States, DS&G, ETL, MET, and UL issue CB certificates. It is a good idea to have the *president's* personal attorney arrange for the initial testing. This makes the results client-privileged information, and the results cannot be used against the company. The attorney hires the outside consultant or laboratory. The initial tests will probably fail, but the product can be reengineered to pass. Remember, under EU regulations, once you *directly hire* a Notified Body, you cannot change Notified Bodies until you obtain compliance.

The new *Good Clinical Practices* (*GCP*) will also eliminate retesting among the members of the International Conference on Harmonization (ICH). This will apply to clinical testing. The chief members of the ICH are the United States, Japan, and the EU. If you run a clinical trial in the United States, you will not have to rerun the trial in the EU in order to obtain certification. The *GCP* sets international standards for clinical trial methods and the report format. It will become law in the EU on July 1, 1997 and is expected to become law in the United States and Japan by the end of 1997.

The 3 Methods of Avoiding Retesting

1. Use a laboratory which has a Memorandum of Understanding with your Notified Body.

2. Use a laboratory which is a member of the CB Scheme.

3. Follow the *Good Clinical Practices*.

The final way you can avoid retesting is to choose a laboratory that has a Memorandum of Understanding (MOU) with your Notified Body. This process applies to all products. You can determine which labs have MOUs by contacting either the Notified Body, a competent consultant in your area, or various professional organizations such as the AAMI.

The first step in obtaining compliance is to read the directives and determine which ones apply to your product. There will be more than one directive

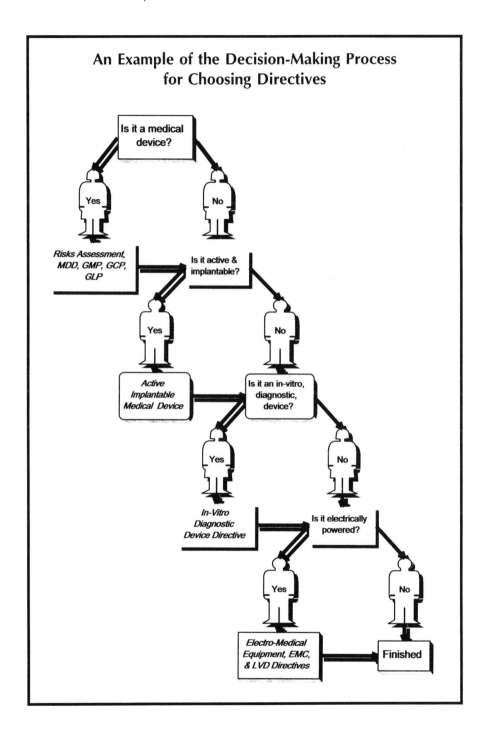

An Example of the Decision-Making Process
for Choosing Directives

Is it a medical device?

Yes

No

Risks Assessment, MDD, GMP, GCP, GLP

Is it active & implantable?

Yes

No

Active Implantable Medical Device

Is it an in-vitro, diagnostic, device?

Yes

No

In-Vitro Diagnostic Device Directive

Is it electrically powered?

Yes

No

Electro-Medical Equipment, EMC, & LVD Directives

Finished

that applies. For example, if you produce a radio-controlled car, you will have to comply not only with the *Toy Safety Directive* but with the *Low Voltage Directive* and the *Electro-Magnetic Compatibility Directive.* You should consult either a competent consultant in your field or a Notified Body to ensure that you are complying with *all* the relevant directives. **Remember, even if you comply with the main directive for your product or service, the CE Marking can still be withheld for not complying with all the appropriate directives.** Your product can be withdrawn from the market if you do not make current copies of all applicable directives and standards available to your employees.

In general, complying with the EU Directives is a simple process. It merely seems complicated because it is unfamiliar. The first step toward compliance is reading and understanding the directives. While you may think of it as a change, 80% of what you are doing now will stay the same. The only major difference is in the documentation. Remember, the directives do not regulate the individual methods you use to produce your product or service. With a good understanding of EU law, you can reap the benefits of EU compliance. For most products or services, complying with the EU Directives will cost less than complying with U.S. law. The process moves much faster in the EU. The following chapters will break down this process in greater detail.

Summary Table for Conformity Assessment

Modules of Conformity Assessment	Conformity Assessment — Product Surveillance		Quality Assurance — Testing			Affixing the CE Marking — Authorization	
	Samples	Each Product	QA Surveillance	EC Type Testing	Technical Documentation	Manufacturer	Third Party
A	O	O			1	■	
B + C	O			■ ISO 9002	2	■	
B + D			■	■ ISO 9002	2	■ ☆	
B + E			■	■ ISO 9003	2	■ ☆	
B + F	■	■			2	■ ☆	■ ☆
G		■			2		■ ☆
H			■	■ ISO 9001	3	■ ☆	

O = supplemental requirements, ■ = action by a third party, ☆ = CE Marking with the Notified Body's identification number, 1 = required to be available, 2 = required by the Notified Body, 3 = part of the quality system.

Procedures for Conformity Assessment Modules During the Design and Production Phase

EC Module		Design		Production	
	Product	Manufacturer	Notified Body	Manufacturer	Notified Body
Module A Internal: Control of Production		• Keeps technical documented • Maintain a TIF file	Module Aa • Intervention of a Notified Body	• Declares conformity with the essential requirements • Affixes the CE Marking	Aa • Performs testing • Performs surveillance
Module B	Module C Conform to Type	• Submits to Notified Body the Technical Documentation • Submits type	• Ascertains conformity with essential requirements • Carries out the required test • Issues EC Type Certificate	• Declares conformity with the approved type • Affixes the CE Marking	• Tests on specific aspects of the product • Produces checks at random intervals
EC Type-Examination	Module D Product Quality Assurance	• Submits to Notified Body the Technical Documentation • Submits type	• Ascertains conformity with essential requirements • Carries out the required test • Issues EC Type Certificate	• ISO 9002 registration • Declares conformity with the approved type • Affixes the CE Marking	• Approves the quality system • Carries out surveillance • Checks the product to type • Declares conformity with the approved type • Affixes the CE Marking

Module	Manufacturer			Notified Body
0 Module E Product Quality Assurance	• Submit to Notified Body the Technical Documentation • Submits type	• Ascertains conformity with essential requirements • Carries out the required test • Issues EC Type Certificate	• ISO 9003 registration • Declares conformity with approved type or essential requirements • Affixes the CE Marking	• Approves the quality system • Carries out surveillance • Type testing
Module F Product Verification	• Submit to Notified Body the Technical Documentation • Submits type	• Ascertains conformity with essential requirements • Carries out the required test • Issues EC Type Certificate	• Declares conformity to approved type or essential requirements • Affixes the CE Marking	• Verifies conformity • Issues certificate of conformity
Module G • Submits Technical Documentation Unit Verification		• Submits unit • Declares conformity • Affixes the CE Marking		• Verifies conformity with essential requirements • Issues Certificate of Conformity
Module H • ISO 9001 • Operates an approved quality system for design Full Quality Assurance		• Operates and approves quality system • Declares conformity • Affixes CE Marking		• Carries out surveillance of the quality system

7

Modules A, B, and C

After choosing the appropriate directives, the next step is to choose which module you will follow. The modules provide a "road map" for compliance. The impact of the individual modules on the directives is usually covered in the annexes of the directive.

Module A

The first module is Module A, Internal Production Control. You comply with this module by self-certifying. This module applies to low-risk items such as lamps, stuffed animals, and most machinery. It applies to the majority of regulated products. However, most services cannot use Module A.

When you use Module A, the first thing you need to do is write your Technical Construction File (TCF).* The purpose of a TCF is to demonstrate to the Competent Authorities that you are in compliance. The TCF must be available to the Competent Authorities, but it does not have to physically reside in the EU. It is usually kept by your authorized representative. *A copy must be kept by the person who places it on the market.* The TCF can be in paper or electronic format. Depending upon the product, there may be guidelines that must be followed for the format of the TCF. Not all products have a specified format. The TCF is used as an assessment tool, to determine if the product is in compliance and covers the design, manufacture, and operation of the product. **The TCF is a confidential document and does not have to be shared with the customer.** The TCF must contain the following:

---

* The TCF is also referred to as the Technical Information File (TIF) in some directives.

Checklist for the TCF

1. Technical drawings
2. Advertising literature
3. Labeling of package and product
4. Instruction manual
5. Results of testing
6. Master list
7. Quality plan
8. Non-conformities plan
9. Address the essential requirements
10. Batch code, etc.
11. Location of standards and directives
12. Designation of signatory

---

1. **General description and complete technical drawings of your product**—You may use photographs to augment your technical drawings, but you cannot substitute photographs for the technical drawings. You also need to include the conceptual design, schematics of subassemblies, circuits, etc.

2. **Complete advertising literature**—You must include descriptions of all variations of advertising that you intend to use. Actual literature or pamphlets that will be handed out must be included. You must fully describe any television or radio advertising that you intend to use. If during the lifetime of the product your advertising changes, you must include the changes in the TCF. However, you do not have to recertify for changes in advertising.

3. **Labeling**—You must include complete copies of all packaging and product labeling. The specific directives will define what must be on the label. At a minimum, it will contain the trade name of the product, the name and address of the manufacturer,

and the CE Marking. It must also include any additional compliance marks required by the directive, for example the ECO-Label (see Chapter 5 for further discussion of compliance marks).

4. **Complete instruction manual**—The instruction manual must explain how to operate the product as well as safety instructions for the user. It must include complete instructions for using the product safely, taking into account the training of the user. It must also have a maintenance schedule and a list of all parts and part numbers. The latest copy of the instruction manual must always be in the TCF. Where appropriate, the instruction manual must include any special conditions or operating hazards as well as:

   a. If the product must work with other products, there must be sufficient detail for the customer to know which product to use.

   b. Information to verify that the product is properly installed.

   c. Any special risks that might arise when in use.

   d. The necessary instructions in the event the package is damaged, especially if sterilization is involved.

   e. Precautions to take if the device requires a chemical to function (for example, hydraulic fluid).

   f. Precautions or unusual risks when disposing of the product.

   g. If the product has a measuring function, you must include methods of calibration and the degree of accuracy.

   h. Instructions for any personal protective equipment needed to use the product.

5. **Results of testing**—All test reports, results of design calculations, and a description of examinations carried out. **This is the most important inclusion in the TCF. It is your physical proof of compliance.**

6. **The master list**—The master list is a list of all changes that have been made either to the product, the manufacturing process, or the literature. The master list can either be in the TCF itself or you can indicate where it is kept.

7. **The quality plan**—It must contain a description or your quality plan. A quality plan shows the process control steps (the points at which you check the product for compliance), the testing schedule, bill of materials (those items that you must purchase to produce the product), method of incoming inspection (you must inspect all incoming raw materials prior to using), and the packaging and shipping process. It also must include anything else that affects the quality of the product.

You can choose to have your supplier inspect the raw materials prior to shipping, but first you must set up a verification system with your supplier. This must be included in your contract with the supplier. You can save a great deal of time and effort if your supplier is already in compliance.

8. **Non-conformities**—You must have a formal plan for detecting and disposing of products that fail your inspection process. You must have checks to ensure that non-conforming products are not inadvertently shipped. This does not mean that you cannot rework non-conforming product. It simply means you must ensure that the non-conforming product does not reach your customers until it conforms.

9. **Essential requirements**—You must show proof that your product meets the essential requirements of the relevant directives.

10. **Batch code**—Where appropriate, you must include a batch code preceded by the word LOT, a serial number, an expiration date, any special storage or handling conditions, warnings or precautions, method of sterilization, and any special operating instructions.

11. **Location**—You must indicate the location of your copies of *all* relevant standards and directives. The Notified Body having a copy does not meet this requirement. These copies must be current.

12. **Signatory**—You must name the person who is designated to be personally responsible for compliance of the product. This is usually the president of the company or the division chief, although it could be the quality manager. It cannot be the person responsible for managing the quality system.

Module A manufacturers are not required to be ISO 9000 registered. However, the EU does expect a quality management system to be in place that follows the ISO 9000 system. You are required to take all necessary steps to ensure your product complies with the *Modules of Conformity Assessment Directive*. This means you must have a quality management system to guarantee that you are producing quality product. For each type of product that you manufacture, there must be a quality plan which specifies what testing will be conducted and to what relevant standards. Whether you become registered or not, an ISO 9000 quality system will help your company prove its compliance to the EU Directives (for more information on ISO 9000 and the EU, see Chapter 10).

After preparing the TCF, the manufacturer issues a Declaration of Conformity. The Declaration of Conformity is a certificate which states that your product is in compliance and lists the relevant directives and standards. The Declaration of Conformity must contain the following:

- Description of the product
- List of the appropriate standards and directives
- Identification of the signatory
- Where appropriate, reference to the EC Type-Examination Certificate issued by a Notified Body

The Declaration of Conformity must accompany the product in its shipping container. It must accompany the product all the way to the individual consumer and may not be removed by a supplier. The Declaration of Conformity will be required for other modules.

The final stage is the application of the CE Marking. The manufacturer affixes the CE Marking and ships it to the customers.

Sample of a Declaration of Conformity

Application of Council Directive(s): _____

Manufacturer's Name: _____

Manufacturer's Address: _____

Name of Equipment: _____

Type No., Model No., or Reference No.: _____

Serial No.: _____

Year of Manufacture: _____

I, the undersigned, hereby declare that the equipment specified above conforms to Directive(s) _____

Place: _____

_____   _____
     Signature (Full Name)   **(Position)**

Date: _____

Harmonized Standard

A technical specification that has been adopted by either CEN or CENELEC. CEN and CENELEC, under their contract with the Commission, have defined the following kinds of harmonized standards.

A standards deal with fundamental concepts. EN 292 for machinery and EN 60601 for electromedical equipment are examples of this category.

B standards deal with general safety aspects of a family of equipment. An example is safety clearance distances (a method of calculation forklift capacity); examples for machinery are EN 294 and EN 563.

B2 standards deal with specific components or devices, such as the EN 60601 series for medical equipment, EN 115 for escalators, and EN 281 for safety devices.

C standards are so-called "vertical" standards covering a single type of machine. EN 670 for manure spreaders is an example.

The designer uses the **A standards** to develop the product specifications. The design review documents the application of the **A standards**, and the results are included in the TCF. The **B and C standards** are the test methods which demonstrate that the product meets the requirements of the relevant directives.

Module Aa Conformity Assessment Procedures

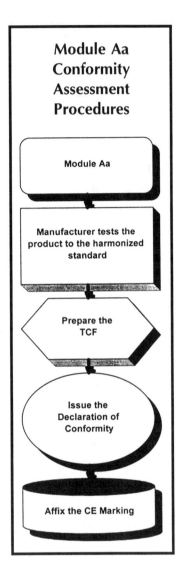

Module Aa

Manufacturer tests the product to the harmonized standard

Prepare the TCF

Issue the Declaration of Conformity

Affix the CE Marking

Module Aa

Module Aa is a combination of Module A and a type-examination. A type-examination is an application of a testing standard. The standard may or may not be harmonized. You must use Module Aa if the product has to be tested, according to the relevant directives and standards. Examples of such products would be electrical plugs, business equipment, or infants' toys. If an EC Type-

Examination is required, it must be done by a Notified Body (see Module B for more information on an EC Type-Examination). If an EC Type-Examination is required, the product or service usually falls under Module C.

Module Aa is usually applied to products such as electrical equipment or components that must have an EU Type Approval (ETA). This procedure is similar to obtaining UL approval in the United States. The C standards will contain information telling you how many samples you must have and what tests you need to run. After obtaining the ETA, the manufacturer performs the surveillance testing and reports the results to the Notified Body for the length of the certification. The length of the certification can be anywhere from three to ten years, depending upon the product. The EU is trying to standardize the time to seven years, but this has not happened yet.

Obtaining Compliance to Module Aa

Mixr's R Us (fictitious name) produces household mixers and blenders. Twenty percent of their sales are in the EU. Their customers have given them a deadline by which to obtain the CE Marking. With fevered energy, the president forms a quality team. Being educated employees, the first thing they do is obtain the relevant directives:

- *Low Voltage Directive* (*LVD*)
- *Electro-Magnetic Compatibility* (*EMC*) *Directive*

They also obtain the *ECO-Label Directive* because one of the main features of their products is that they have been redesigned to be energy efficient.

After reading the directives, they then determine what standards apply to their products by reading the Council Decisions of the individual directives:

The *LVD* harmonized standards that apply are 261-1 through 4, AMI to HD 281 S1, EN 50084, EN 60065, EN 600335-2-14, EN 60730-1, and EN 60730-AMI 1 through 12. From the *EMC,* the standards are EN 61000-3-2 and EN 50082-1.

As part of setting up the quality plan, they decide to perform the bulk of the testing in-house. However, based on legal counsel, they decide to have a representative sample tested by a Notified Body to ensure that their in-house testing is accurate. In discussion with the Notified Body, they discover that they can treat all of their mixers as a family of products and reduce the amount of testing necessary.

After the products successfully pass the tests, they prepare their TCF and the Declaration of Conformity.

Module B

Module B is the EC Type-Examination. It is always used with another module. The term "type" is used to mean a representative sample* of a product. It may refer to more than one sample. It cannot be a prototype or a product made in the pilot stage. You must be formally in production or convince the Notified Body that your prototype is exactly like the production sample, which can be extremely difficult to do. The TCF accompanies the sample to the Notified Body. The Notified Body reviews the TCF for compliance and performs the examination. The TCF should enable the Notified Body to determine if your manufactured product will meet the essential requirements of the directives. (For more information on the TCF, see Module A.)

An EC Type-Examination can refer to a family of products under certain directives. As an example, a heating pad with several different sizes would be a family of products. A single set of test results could be used to place the entire family on the market. After choosing your type, you must have it tested to one of the harmonized standards listed for the relevant directive. After the product passes the testing, the Notified Body will disseminate the information to the other Notified Bodies and the Competent Authorities. **However, the information is confidential and will not be given to your customers or competitors.** It is not public domain information. The information will be kept on file for ten years after the last product is produced.

After receiving your Certificate of Conformity Assessment, any changes made to the product will have to go back to the Notified Body for approval. This certificate is your proof that the product passed the appropriate testing, and it must be placed in your TCF. A copy is also sent with the product, and the identification number of the Notified Body will be placed next to your CE Marking. You must submit a description of the changes, and the Notified Body will determine if you need to have the product retested. Any changes must be submitted, even minor ones. For example, if your electric plug has always been black and you want to make it orange, you must submit this change. These additional approvals will be affixed to the original Certificate of Conformity Assessment.

After your product successfully passes the testing, you need to choose another module. Module B is unique in that it is never used alone. It only refers to the

---

* The term "representative sample" is interpreted in the EU to mean a statistically selected sample.

testing of products. Depending upon the directive and the degree of risk, it can be a single test of a representative sample or on-site surveillance testing. If you require on-site surveillance, you will have to comply with Module C or above.

Module C

Module C is a combination of self-declaration and the EC Type-Examination. First, you prepare your TCF (for further discussion, see Module A). The foundation of Module C is the quality plan, which will be reviewed by the Notified Body. The purpose of the quality plan is to ensure that the product is in compliance with the relevant directives. The quality plan details what testing is to be performed, when in the manufacturing phase the testing is to be performed, and which Notified Body will do it. The testing is your proof of compliance to the harmonized standards. It must be done whenever necessary in the manufacturing process to prove that the product is safe and meets the standards. Product testing is frequently confused with implementation of the quality system. In many American manufacturing plants, the only test for quality is the final product testing/inspection. In the EU, they are two separate issues. If you must have on-site surveillance testing done, it can be done either by a Notified Body reviewing your testing processes and results and/or the Notified Body periodically testing your products. The higher the degree of risk to health, safety, and

---

An Example of a Module C Company

EXACT is a company (fictitious) that supplies force calibrators to fit industrial equipment. It is a service company and needs to comply with Module C. These are components under EU law; therefore, manufacturers do not have to obtain a Certificate of Compliance. However, EXACT must obtain one for its calibrators because it is going to incorporate them into a customer's machinery.

EXACT's calibrators are in compliance with the *Metrology Directives,* the *Instrument Directive,* the *LVD,* and the *EMC.* If they are going into a potentially explosive atmosphere, they will have to comply with the *PEA* as well.

The standards from the *EMC* are EN 50065-1, EN 55011, and EN 61000-3-2. The harmonized standards from the *LVD* are HD 301 S1 and HD 324 S1. Because the *Metrology* and *Instrument Directives* are older, there are no harmonized standards currently.

Module C
Conformity Assessment Procedure

the environment, the more likely the Notified Body will perform both types of surveillance testing. For example, if you produce a motor for use in a light industrial environment, the Notified Body will review your test processes and results. However, if the motor is used in mining equipment, the Notified Body will review your data and perform testing.

The definition of what must be included in a quality plan is in ISO 9000–4 and IEC 301. Implementation of a quality plan requires the following steps:

1. Management commitment—The necessary resources and leadership must be committed to the project. The more you do in-house, the more money you will save. However, the trade-off is between money and time. For most regulated products, the clock is already ticking.

2. Management formation of a Steering Committee to plan the compliance program—The Steering Committee is responsible for:
   a. Reviewing the relevant directives.
   b. Selecting the appropriate standards.
   c. Implementing the testing verification program—The testing verification program ensures that your product will pass the EC Type-Examination prior to going to the Notified Body. This is important because under EU law, any testing by a Notified Body is subject to review by the Competent Authorities. Technically, if your product fails the EC Type-Examination, the Competent Authority can withdraw your product from the market. All products should be tested in-house first.

3. Selecting the Notified Body—You should consult your customers to see if they have a preference. You will find that many do. You also must ensure that the Notified Body you choose is listed for the relevant directives. Since you must use a Notified Body for each specific directive that applies, you may have to use more than one, depending upon your product. For example, if you make a stamping press, it must be tested by a Notified Body for the *Machinery Directive* and by one for the *PEA*, the *LVD*, and the *EMC*. Some Notified Bodies do overlap directives, and this is where good research can pay off. Remember, you cannot change Notified Bodies after you have hired one; therefore, a great deal of thought should be given to which one you hire. This will be a long-term relationship, lasting at least two years.

4. Meeting with the Notified Body—
   a. Define the testing plan. The testing plan is where you decide what tests you will run, sample size, frequency of testing, and the for-

mat of reporting results. This is decided jointly with the Notified Body, according to the requirements in the test standards.

b. Arrange for the EC Type-Examination (see Module B for more information)

5. Begin the implementation training with your work force. The necessary steps are as follows:

a. Introduction—You need to have a brief overview for management and employees. That way, everyone understands what needs to be done and how it will be done.

b. Select two employees for internal auditor training—This enables you to audit your system in-house, prior to the actual audits, to check on your level of compliance. These employees also become valuable resources for answering questions during the implementation and maintenance phases. *The success of your quality program hinges on the performance of the internal auditors. If the internal auditors are helpful, and the benefits can be sold to the employees, there is no limit to the achievements that can be accomplished.*

c. Select two personnel for EU Directive requirements and documentation training. These personnel will be in charge of writing your compliance documentation and keeping it current. Their main job will be preparing the TCF. For small companies, this does not have to be a full-time position, but for large companies, it should be.

6. Start the procedure documentation, job descriptions, and work instructions. How much you need to do will depend upon how much you have already done. You must make sure that all documentation is consistent with your quality plan. This ensures that you can prove your product or service is in compliance. If the Competent Authorities decide to check your product for compliance, they will expect to see all of this documentation. If your product is withdrawn from the market, your legal defense comes from these documents.

7. Review the quality manual and quality plan. At this point, you need to make sure that the quality manual matches the quality plan and include any changes. Your quality plan must match your manufacturing process. It must reflect what your are doing, not what you are planning to do. You are not required to obtain ISO 9000 registration for a Module C product; however, the directives will state that you must have a quality system (see Chapter 10 for more information on ISO 9000).

8. Train all personnel in the quality system.

9. Prepare the TCF. Decide the format and location you will use. Also, at this point you must decide who will be your authorized representative and signatory (for further information on the signatory, see Declaration of Conformity under Module A). The authorized representative is located in the EU and acts as your agent before all regulatory bodies of the EU. This person does not have to be an EU citizen; he or she must simply reside in the EU. Usually, your authorized representative is your distributor in Europe. He or she prepares the documentation that is shipped with the product to the customer (you still need to prepare the documentation that goes to the authorized representative), translates the information into the various languages, and double checks the documentation and labeling for compliance.

10. Receive the Certificate of Conformity Assessment—The Notified Body issues this document after the testing is complete and your product has passed the testing. If your product fails the test, you must start over. That is why your verification testing program is so important.

11. Affix the CE Marking, and issue the Declaration of Conformity—and schedule the celebration!

Once your product is in compliance, your work is not done. You must still conduct frequent checks of your product and place continual status reports in your TCF. Also, the TCF must contain compliance reviews and disposition of non-conformities. The EU requires continual compliance.

The implementation steps are the same for every company; the differences are in the specific requirements of the relevant directives. The basic steps in implementing Module C are the same, whether for a manufacturer or a service provider. The best insurance for obtaining and remaining in compliance is good management commitment. Remember, the purpose of this system is to document and demonstrate compliance. Doing it after your product is pulled from the market for non-conformities is too late.

8

Modules D and E

Module D

Module D is product quality assurance. Products or services with a higher degree of risk must apply this module. Examples are a Class IIa medical device or a service company doing engineering design. The difference between Module C and Module D is that in Module D you are required to become ISO 9001/2 registered.* After placing the CE Marking, the identification numbers of all Notified Bodies are placed next to the CE Marking, and the Certificate of Compliance accompanies the product to the consumer.

A Module D Company

Auto Designs, Inc. (fictitious name) designs components for automobiles. It has developed a 3-D structure modeling software package for determination of the structural integrity and performance of a component in service. The company also performs dynamic testing to verify results and sometimes produces prototypes for clients, but only in small volumes. Because its reputation is growing in the international marketplace, the company has become ISO 9001 registered. It then decides to obtain the CE Marking as well.

Auto Designs decides to follow Module D, because some of these components must have EC Type-Examinations by a Notified Body. As part of its service, the company arranges for the testing, interprets the results, and assists in the preparation of the TCF for its customers.

---

* *The EU Modules for Conformity Assessment Directives* and *The EU Certification and Technical Standards Directives,* St. Lucie Press, 1997.

Elements of an ISO 9000 Quality System

Title	9001 Section #	9002 Section #
Management Responsibility	4.1	4.1
Quality System Principles	4.2	4.2
Contract Review	4.3	4.3
Design Control	4.4	none
Document & Data Control	4.5	4.5
Purchasing	4.6	4.6
Control of Customer-Supplied Product	4.7	4.7
Product ID & Traceability	4.8	4.8
Process Control	4.9	4.9
Inspection & Testing	4.10	4.10
Control of Inspection	4.11	4.11
Inspection & Test Status	4.12	4.12
Control of Non-Conforming Products	4.13	4.13
Corrective & Preventive Actions	4.14	4.14
Handling, Storage, Packaging & Delivery	4.15	4.15
Control of Quality Records	4.16	4.16
Internal Quality Audits	4.17	4.17
Training	4.18	4.18
Service	4.19	4.19
Statistical Techniques	4.20	4.20

ISO 9001/2 registration may not be done by just anyone. **Your certification must be issued by a Notified Body listed in the** *Official Journal of the European Communities* **for the relevant directives.** Notified Bodies are accredited by a Competent Authority who uses the EN 45000 series to accredit them for a specific directive. There are no restrictions placed on who you can hire to prepare you for the certification audit.

The ISO 9000 quality system must:

1. Include a quality manual which:
   a. Assigns responsibility for implementing and maintaining the quality system
   b. Authorizes the execution of responsibility
2. State the organization's structure, responsibility, and the powers of management

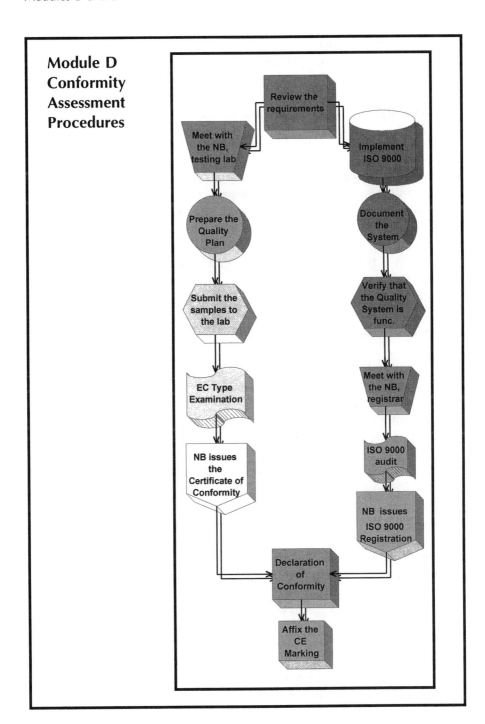

**Module D
Conformity
Assessment
Procedures**

3. Document the manufacturing process, quality assurance, and the systematic actions for operating the quality system
4. Contain quality plans for the products
5. Contain quality records
6. Specify the monitoring methods for assuring compliance

Remember, the purpose of the quality system is to ensure continual compliance of the product.

Surveillance of the quality system and the product or service is the responsibility of the Notified Body that registered your quality system. The Notified Body will not conduct the EC Type-Examination surveillance, but will double check that it is done. EC Type-Examination surveillance is the formal surveillance testing to check that the product is still in compliance. It is done by the same Notified Body that issued your original Certificate of Conformity. The Notified Body will audit your quality system at least twice a year. In product surveillance testing, the Notified Body will probably not run all the tests necessary for the EC Type-Examination surveillance. For example, in the medical device field, a Notified Body may only test to see if the product was sterilized properly.

For Module D products, all field failures usually have to be reported to the Notified Body and/or the Competent Authorities. If a product malfunctions after the consumer receives it, you must also generate a report identifying the cause, why it failed, and a proposed plan for correcting the non-conformity. If the cause is the manufacturing process, you must correct the manufacturing process. You may also have to recall all your products in the field, depending upon the requirements of the individual directives. The Notified Body will tell you if this is necessary. If a design flaw caused the malfunction, then you will have to recertify your product or service. If you do not correct the problem, the Competent Authority will probably withdraw your product from the market. The non-conformity surveillance and reporting will continue for up to seven years after the last product is manufactured.

If you are in a situation in which you can use either Module C or Module D, there are two advantages to picking Module D. First, if you are ISO 9000 registered, you can do more of the testing in-house. This will save you money when you reach the surveillance phase. The second is the liability protection. In most courts, the third-party system grants you greater liability protection. In the EU, ISO 9000 registration is taken to mean that you have done *everything* possible to ensure compliance, which means that your liability will probably be reduced under the law (for more benefits of ISO 9000, see Chapters 4 and 10).

Module E

Module E is called Product Quality Assurance. Module E products only have to undergo final inspection. This module is restricted to repackagers, contract assemblers, and sterilizers. A repackager is a company that buys a product and

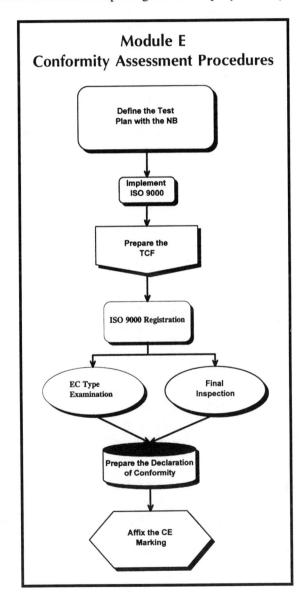

either resells it under its own name or packages it as a subcontractor. An example would be IV bags, where one company produces the IV solution and the IV bags and gives it to the repackager, who places the solution into the bags. The contract assembler builds a product for another company, which places its logo on the product. Contract assemblers do not buy the components or design products. They simply manufacture products for clients. If you are a subcontractor and you purchase raw materials, you cannot use Module E.

Module E companies must be ISO 9001/2/3 registered and must have an EC Type-Examination performed by a Notified Body.* They follow the testing procedures of either Module C, D, or E. Which one will depend upon the directives and standards to which your product must be in compliance. Again, the higher the risk to the health and safety of EU citizens and to the environment, the more likely it is you will have to follow the testing procedures of Module E. Very few products or services will be able to apply Module E.

A Module E Company

Hard 'N' R (fictitious name) is a commercial heat treater. Because its customers export to Europe, Hard 'N' R becomes in compliance with the EU Directives. The company heat treats products that are used in the medical and transportation fields. It first becomes ISO 9003 registered because it only has to certify the final results of the heat treatments. Some of these products have to be sent to a Notified Body to be tested. Hard 'N' R supplies its products to its customers with a Certificate of Conformity Assessment and a Declaration of Conformity. This helps customers obtain product certification more quickly. Because of this benefit of its service, Hard 'N' R actually picks up some of its competitors' customers. Because the company treats its products as families of products, its TCF is generic. Using company software and a LAN system, Hard 'N' R has an individual quality plan for each of its customers' products. It makes the electronic database available to its customers (again, so they can obtain certification more quickly) and the Competent Authorities. The increase in customers pays for the cost of compliance within the first six months. Hard 'N' R expects its business to double over the next three years. Also, the company loses fewer customers for two reasons. The first is because of the benefits of using a service in compliance. The reason is that customers that change heat treaters must recertify their products because Hard 'N' R's CE Marking is stamped into the product along with the customer's.

---

* *The EU Modules for Conformity Assessment Directives* and *The EU Certification and Technical Standards Directives,* St. Lucie Press, 1997.

9

Modules F, G, and H

Module F

Module F is also called Product Verification. The difference between Module D and Module F is that the degree of risk of the product or service is higher in Module F. Module F products may require verification at as high as the 95% confidence level, depending upon the product. Module F products are products for which the Member States require certification before they can be placed into service. They are always large volume products, such as automotive safety components, gas-fired hot-water heaters, boilers, etc. In Module F, you must have an EC Type-Examination by a Notified Body, become ISO 9000 registered by a Notified Body, and prepare a TCF.* You cannot place the CE Marking until you receive your Certificate of Conformity Assessment from both Notified Bodies (the one that audits your quality system and the one that does your EC Type-Examination). The identification numbers of the Notified Bodies are placed next to your CE Marking.

For example, if your company designs bumpers for automobiles, you have to follow Module F, because the bumper is considered an essential safety component. Every design would go through a design verification process in which you have to demonstrate that your design software package works and is accurate when compared with real-life testing. You will also have to design a prototype bumper, install it on a vehicle, and have it tested to prove that it meets the standards and the essential requirements of the directives. Other

---

* *The EU Modules for Conformity Assessment Directives* and *The EU Certification and Technical Standards Directives,* St. Lucie Press, 1997.

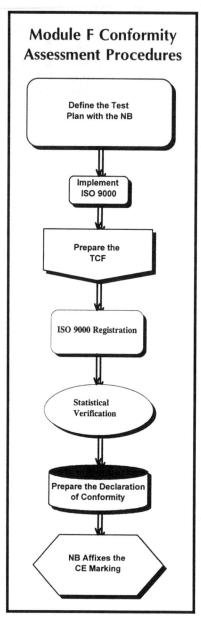

Module F Conformity Assessment Procedures

- Define the Test Plan with the NB
- Implement ISO 9000
- Prepare the TCF
- ISO 9000 Registration
- Statistical Verification
- Prepare the Declaration of Conformity
- NB Affixes the CE Marking

examples of Module F products are aeronautical equipment, safety components of machines, and mining equipment.

If the product type is such that its quality cannot be determined by a series of end point tests, then a statistical process control and process verification will have to be developed. This is called Statistical Verification, which is the process of using statistical procedures to ensure that a batch or continuous process is in compliance with its requirements. It is continuous, ongoing testing. The entire manufacturing process is tested, from the quality of the raw materials to the final end product. The spot checks on the product during manufacturing are statistically selected. The procedures for statistically selecting the samples and the sample sizes are in the individual standards. The manufacturer must provide homogenous lots for testing. Products in a sample lot must be individually examined and appropriate tests performed on each sample. You are testing every stage of the manufacturing process and proving that the end product is in compliance with the directives. The documentation resulting from the statistical process control demonstrates compliance to the quality requirements. Process Verification is the analysis of your statistical documentation, data, and the EC Type-Examination that proves that the product meets its specific requirements under the EU Directives. Note that the biggest mistake made in statistical process control is that no one ever reviews the control charts and outputs. The corrective action sections of ISO 9001/2 (Sections 4.9, 4.10, and 4.14) require that management reviews the results to improve process performance and to

---

A Module F Company

A company that makes gas hot-water heaters sells its products in Europe. It must comply with Module F because each hot-water tank must be certified by a Notified Body. The Notified Body elects to use statistical process control because of the size of the lots.

The company is ISO 9001 registered, which means it can do most of the testing in-house. The Notified Body is only doing a final test, rather than testing every product during every stage of production. The Notified Body does periodically review the in-house testing program and reviews all test results.

The company ships a lot of hot-water heaters (after testing all of the heaters in-house) to its authorized representative in the EU. The authorized representative arranges with the Notified Body to select a representative sample for the EC Type-Examination. The Notified Body then does the testing and releases the lot for marketing. At that point, the authorized representative labels the hot-water heater with the appropriate compliance symbols.

---

reduce or eliminate non-conformities. Ongoing review of the testing program can save you a tremendous amount of money in reducing operational costs. It also enables you to plan for necessary product design and manufacturing process changes. **The EU expects you to prevent non-conformities whenever possible.**

Normally, the manufacturer sends a lot to the authorized representative in the EU, who then arranges for testing by the Notified Body. The Notified Body then affixes its identification symbol to each product and draws up a Certificate of Conformity. All the products that pass the testing may then be placed on the market. If an entire lot is rejected, the Notified Body, in conjunction with the manufacturer, is responsible for ensuring that the lot is not placed on the market. If there is frequent production of rejected lots, the Notified Body will require correction of the manufacturing process and possibly withdrawal of the CE Marking.

Module G

Module G is Unit Verification and is used for customized, single-unit products or services, such as a chemical reactor, industrial food equipment, or a plant construction project. This is the catchall module. If none of the other modules apply, Module G is used. These products are usually single items or products made in small volumes. The difference between Module F and Module G is the number of units. Module F covers multiple units. Module G products are produced in such small volumes that statistics are not accurate. Depending on the unit, ISO 9000 quality system registration may be required and the unit may require an EC Type-Examination.* The TCF normally accompanies the unit and becomes part of the plant's documentation.

Generally, a Notified Body will run an approval test and check conformity, either by off-site testing of components or by testing the entire process on-site. This will depend on not only the type of product, but also on its size and complexity. Because these products are customized and unique, there is no standardized EU technical approval standard. Each EC Type-Examination must be crafted for each product. It is quite possible that you will have to meet several directives and standards. Individual components, as well as the whole product, may also have to be certified and bear the CE Marking. The testing of these products is usually quite complicated and requires a great deal of coordination.

Construction projects, such as building a production line or an entire plant, also fall under Module G. The primary contractor is responsible for obtaining the CE Marking. This applies to production lines in the EU and may also apply to ones outside the EU if the manufacturer sells its products in Europe. The customer will usually request the Unit Verification based upon individual needs.

When producing a unit that will be used in the EU, the primary directives are the *Worker's Safety Directives*, no matter what the unit is. While these directives are written to apply to the actual user and owner of the machine, the equipment must be manufactured to meet the essential requirements of these directives. In some cases, the equipment may even have to be tested while in use at its intended location for certification. The CE Marking alone may not be sufficient.

There is a difference between a type-examination and an EC type-examination. An EC Type-Examination is always Module B, which is a product test. A type-examination can be Module C, Product Quality Assurance (Module D or E), Product Verification (Module F), Unit Verification (Module G), or Full Quality Assurance (Module H). As you progress through the modules, the

---

* *The EU Modules for Conformity Assessment Directives* and *The EU Certification and Technical Standards Directives,* St. Lucie Press, 1997.

A Module G Company

Fat Treats, Inc. (fictitious name) hires a contractor to add a new potato chip line to its plant in Ireland. Because the potato chip line will have to be customized to fit Fat Treats, Inc.'s factory, Module G must be followed. The company that designs the line will have to take into account the plant size, the amount of potato chips to be produced per day, the type of potatoes used, the type of oil used to fry the chips, and compatibility with existing packaging equipment.

The experienced contractor has a food equipment manufacturer that is already in compliance with relevant directives. This will save time when obtaining the CE Marking for the new line. The contractor is also ISO 9001 registered. He signs a contract with a Notified Body to perform the type-examination. He does not have to repeat the EC Type-Examination on the machinery, because that has already been done by his manufacturer. The Notified Body will verify that the line meets its designed capacity of 2,000 kg/hr and the relevant safety and food directives and standards.

Following a design review with the Notified Body, the Declaration of Design Conformity is obtained and the equipment is ordered and installed. The Notified Body inspects the line on-site and verifies the performance. Then, the Notified Body issues the Certificate of Conformity. The company accepts the line and writes the operating manual, trains the personnel, and puts the line into service.

---

testing and certification become more complicated. Module G products have to apply Module B (EC Type-Examination), but they also require Unit Verification performed by a Notified Body. In Unit Verification, you must test to see that a unit functions as intended in its intended environment. It is a system verification. In an EC Type-Examination, only the individual product is tested to determine if it is in compliance. Unit Verification usually involves several EC Type-Examinations. First, each component goes through an EC Type-Examination; then the entire unit undergoes Unit Verification. The process can be very simple or very complex, depending upon the customized unit.

Whether or not you have to become ISO 9001 registered depends upon the directives with which you must comply. However, it is unlikely that you can choose not to obtain ISO 9001 registration because of the complexity of your type of product. If you do have a choice, obtaining ISO 9001 registration makes obtaining Unit Verification much simpler. "Under ISO 9001, the manufacturer submits the full quality system for approval, a preferable alternative to the more intrusive [EU] process of continuously submitting representative samples to a third-party for screening."* In the case of a large unit, such as a plant, ISO 14000 registration may also be required.

The TCF will contain all drawings and schematics, the quality manual for the unit, the operational manual, the safety manual, and the work instructions. Particular emphasis should be placed on safely operating the unit. The TCF file will be much more complex than one written an for individual product. It will contain the instruction and safety manuals for every individual component. However, there still must be one cohesive operating manual. It must document every step in the process. The customer is usually responsible for writing the cohesive operating manual from the information provided by the builder. This is one case where the TCF resides with the customer rather than the manufacturer. You will save yourself a great deal of time and effort if you purchase components that already have the CE Marking.

The Notified Body reviews the design requirements and specifications to determine if the unit will meet its intended purpose. If the Notified Body feels it will, it issues a Declaration of Design Conformity. The Declaration of Design Conformity has two purposes. First, it gives a "green light" to building the unit, and second, it verifies that the components of the unit conform to the EU requirements. The Notified Body will concentrate primarily on the worker safety aspect of the unit, asking whether the unit is safe to operate. After receiving the Declaration, you can order the parts and begin construction. Not all Module G products need a Declaration of Design Conformity. It depends upon the product and its use. The relevant standards will tell you if you need a Declaration.

While building the unit, the Notified Body may wish to test each component as it is installed. The Notified Body will definitely review and inspect the unit when it is complete. After the unit has passed the final inspection, the Notified Body issues a Certificate of Conformity to the primary contractor. The contractor then issues a Declaration of Conformity. Both the Certificate of Conformity and the Declaration of Conformity will reside with the unit. The customer and the primary contractor will both have originals. These documents must be kept on file for ten years past the date the unit was last used. The primary contractor places the CE Marking on the unit, along with the identification symbols of all Notified Bodies that were involved in the conformity assessment procedures. Each component or piece of equipment must also have a CE Marking, along with the identification symbol of the Notified Body that assessed the particular piece.

---

* *The ISO 9000 Handbook,* CEEM Information Services, Chicago, 1992, p. 235.

Module H

Module H is called Full Quality Assurance. This module covers products with the highest degree of risk. Class III medical devices and airplane motors are examples of products in this module. If failure of the product or service could result in death, serious injury, or environmental damage, it probably falls under Module H. A very small number of products fall under Module H.

You must be ISO 9001 registered, with your quality system audits conducted by a Notified Body,* and your quality system must include design verification and design control procedures. This ensures that your design per-

---

A Module H Company

Perfect Beat (fictitious name) is a company that produces pacemakers (a Class III medical device which must comply with Module H). The company hires a Notified Body to perform the EC Type-Examination and the Full Quality Assurance Type-Examination. The Notified Body was recommended by most of Perfect Beat's distributors in the EU and has the added benefit of being able to perform both examinations.

The first step is implementation of the Full Quality Assurance System using the *AIMD,* ISO 9001, and EN 46001. The implementation team prepares representative samples for the qualification testing according to the following standards:

- EN 30993-3 through 6
- EN 602-2-10

The clinical trial, following the format of the new *GCP,* has already been conducted. The following guidelines were used for meeting the essential requirements:

EN 556, EN 60601-1, EN 60601-1-1 and, EN 60601-1-2

The team sets up an internal audit system, training, and product testing. Working with the Notified Body, Perfect Beat achieves certification. Every product shipped to the EU was tested by the Notified Body and certified before being placed on the market. Because of its well-planned internal surveillance system, with its emphasis on corrective action and continuous improvement, Perfect Beat lowers its rate of non-conformities.

---

* *The EU Modules for Conformity Assessment Directives* and *The EU Certification and Technical Standards Directives,* St. Lucie Press, 1997.

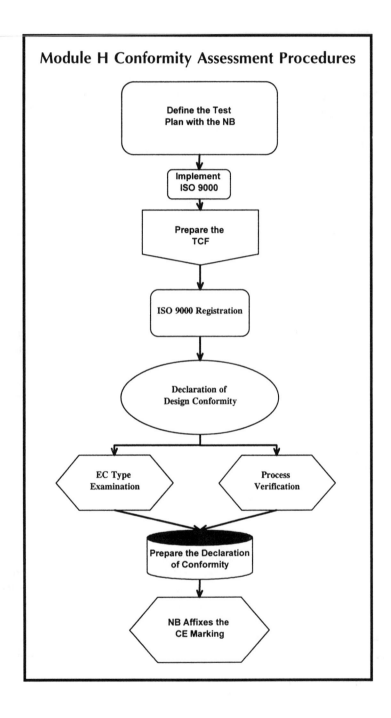

forms as intended. The Notified Body will test your products before, during, and after manufacturing and will also determine how often these tests are conducted. You cannot change the design or the process without prior approval of the Notified Body, which will issue a new Declaration of Design Conformity prior to implementing the change. The Notified Body evaluates the proposed change to determine whether the product still complies with the original Declaration of Conformity or whether it must go through the entire conformity assessment procedure again.

The major difference between Module H and the other modules is design verification. Statistical verification may also be required for this module. The manufacturer must file a formal application with the Notified Body for the design verification. The application should contain sufficient information for the product to be understood and to establish conformity with the essential requirements. The application must contain:

1. Design specifications, including the standards that apply.
2. Design calculations and the results of tests carried out to demonstrate compliance. The EC Type-Examination on the prototype must have already been done, and the results of that testing are included in the application.

The application follows the format of the TCF. After examining the application, the Notified Body issues a Certificate of Design Conformity. Along with the certificate, the manufacturer receives the necessary information for identifying the approved design. The application and data are also forwarded to the Competent Authorities and other Notified Bodies. The final CE Marking on the product will include the data supplied by the Notified Body and its identification number. The date of manufacture, commercial name, technical standards, and a certificate number for the Certificate of Design Conformity also must be included with the CE Marking.

The quality system will place greater emphasis on an adequate description and verification of the system. While ISO 9001 surveillance audits usually take place every six months, they are more frequent for Module H products. Also, depending upon the product, the Notified Body may perform an EC Type-Examination on every product. For example if you produce heart-lung bypass machines, every machine will undergo an EC Type-Examination. This greatly increases the liability protection for the manufacturer.

EC surveillance is conducted on the quality system and the results are formally reported to the Commission. EC surveillance requirements are stated in the directives. EC surveillance gives the Notified Body the power to inspect your entire plant whenever it feels it is necessary. The Notified Body inspects the designs, manufacturing process, testing, storage, quality system documentation, quality records (with particular attention paid to the results of analysis and testing), inspection reports, test data, calibration data, qualification reports of the personnel involved, and anything else which may impact the quality of the product and provides an audit report to the manufacturer. The Notified Body may also conduct unannounced inspection visits, in which tests may be carried out to check the proper functioning of the quality system. The Notified Body provides a report of this visit to the manufacturer as well.

If a non-conformity is discovered, it will require corrective action. Normally, the Notified Body will schedule a reinspection, by which time the problem must be fixed. If it is not, the Notified Body must report it to the Competent Authority, which will pass the problem on to the Standing Committee. At this point, your product will be withdrawn from the market within 15 days. You do have the right to appeal directly to the Standing Committee, but most likely you will need to have your system and product recertified. The minimum amount of time your product will be off the market is six months. This is why an ongoing, in-house surveillance audit and testing program is so essential under the EU system.

10

ISO 9000 and the EU Quality System

Harmonization of Directives and Standards

In the 1979 *Cassis de Dijon* case, the Court ruled that Member States could not erect technical barriers to the free movement of goods. Then, in 1985, the Court ordered the Council to implement the ruling in the *Cassis de Dijon* case. The Council had been dragging its feet up until then. The EU Council responded by passing the *Outline for Harmonization Directive* in 1985 (see Appendix 1). The Outline established a plan for creating "New Approach Directives" and harmonized standards. Directive 91/C287/EEC and Directive 85/C136/01 form the *Outline for Harmonization Directive* for the European Union. This directive defines the approach that the EU is going to take to unify the technical regulations among the member countries.

The *Outline for Harmonization Directive* states that the Council wishes to standardize technical regulations so that products can be marketed freely within the EU. However, the Council emphasizes that the safety and health of the public must continue to be protected.

The member countries agree to monitor the technical regulations in order to ensure that those regulations that are unnecessary are removed. The Member States also agree to recognize products manufactured which conform to EU Directives and to allow those products to be sold in their countries.

The power to draw up the necessary technical standards is given to those authorities who are competent in the particular technical field. Once a new harmonized standard is published in the *Official Journal of the European*

Communities, and the Member States have transposed the applicable directive into law, the producers must meet these standards. These harmonized standards are voluntary; however, a manufacturer that chooses not to follow these standards must prove that the product still conforms to the essential requirements of the directives that apply. The standards become mandatory when a manufacturer chooses them. A system of committees is set up to ensure that this approach functions.

The European Commission also outlines in 91/C287/EEC the main elements and the principles that should be used to write directives. All directives should address safety of the public, free movement of goods, and conformity.

CEN and CENELEC are defined as the EU standards organization for harmonized standards. The International Organization for Standardization (ISO) has final authority on any standards with which it chooses to become involved. Usually, CENELEC handles electrical standards, CEN handles non-electrical ones, and ISO handles international, generic, broad-based standards. The Standing Committee for a directive supervises the Technical Advisory Group (TAG) which develops the standards. A TAG is a subcommittee of a standards organization. The Competent Authorities are responsible for regulating the standard.

Audit Standards

ISO 10005	Guidelines for Quality Plans (prIEC 301-2)
ISO 10007	Guidelines for Configuration Management (prIEC 301-3)
ISO 10011-1	Auditing
ISO 10011-2	Qualification Criteria for Auditors
ISO 10011-3	Management of Audit Programs
ISO 10012-1	Metrological Conformation for Measuring Equipment
ISO 10013	Guidelines for Quality Manuals

Note: This is the EU EN 45000 series

This directive also gives the Notified Bodies their power to issue the CE Marking. These Notified Bodies must carry out their duties in accordance with ISO guidelines. The Member States are responsible for regulating all Notified Bodies within their borders.

Development of ISO 9000

In 1985, the Council also asked ISO to develop a generic quality management system. ISO developed the ISO 9000 Quality Management System. ISO 9000 was based upon the ECC Pattern Type Approval* and military standards. Both had been around for over 20 years. The Council felt that one system was needed to ensure free movement of goods. The multiple systems in use at that time were proving to be a major barrier to the transfer of goods and services within the EU. The Council felt that the principles of quality were independent of the product. Quality was quality whether you made stuffed animals or computers.

Development of Harmonized Standards

The Council developed the harmonized standards for the same reason the ISO 9000 quality system was developed. National standards were creating another barrier to the free movement of goods. Each country had its own standards for the testing of products. The Council decided to standardize these testing measures. The Council also stated that from now on, Member States had to mutually recognize national standards in areas where harmonized standards did not exist yet. In the event of conflict between the standards and the directives, the directives are the final authority.

Development of the EU Compliance System

The EU Council concluded that the American method of compliance control, in which you regulate every single product and step in the manufacturing process and then have the government audit you, was expensive and ineffective. The individual Member States had used this system for 30 years as well.

The Council decided to develop a better system, one that was more effective and lowered the cost of governmental compliance monitoring. It started by examining the reasons for a compliance system (protect the health, safety, and environment of EU citizens) and then developed a system which met this requirement. The Council also wanted a generic system that did not need to be changed to meet technology advances. It developed a system which had three cornerstones:

---

* The *Instrument Directive* (71/316/EEC) established the ECC Pattern Type Approval. A Notified Body tests and audits an instrument manufacturer to ensure that his instrument yields accurate measurements. This is required for all instruments used in commercial transactions such as scales, flow meters, etc.

Hierarchy of Conformity Assessment

CE Marking

1. Harmonized standards and directives
2. Independent third-party audit system, paid for by the manufacturer or service provider
3. Control of the inputs and a quality management system to ensure that the manufacturing processes are functioning properly.

The generic system would be based upon the degree of risk associated with a product or service. The Council did not want to regulate areas that did not need regulation. The greater the risk, the greater the compliance requirements. It then ranked the different product areas and prioritized by starting with the areas of greatest risk. The Council gave the list to the Commission and ordered it to develop these directives by January 1, 1993. Toys was the first area tackled. These directives have been developed with a great deal of involvement from industry as well as the EU government.

Most of the harmonized directives are no longer in the transition period, but are now in effect. Over 98% of the "New Approach Directives" and harmonized standards have been transposed by the Member States into law. With the implementation of the Custom Union, most of the regulatory system is functional. It will be fully functional by the end of 1997. Custom inspections are still being developed.

The EU Quality Management System

The purpose of the quality system in the EU is to verify that the product or service meets the essential requirements of the relevant directives. The EU requires the direct involvement of management. Even if your product does not

ISO 9000 Quality Management Standards

ISO 8402   Vocabulary
ISO 9000-1   Guidelines for selection and use
ISO 9002-2   Generic guidelines for the application of ISO 9001/2/3
ISO 9000-3   Guidelines for the application of ISO 9001 to software
ISO 9000-4   Guidelines for dependable program management (IEC 301-1)
ISO 9001   Model for quality assurance in design, development, production, installation, and service
ISO 9002   Model for quality assurance in production, installation, and service
ISO 9003   Model for quality assurance in final inspection
ISO 9004-1   Guidelines
ISO 9004-2   Guidelines for service
ISO 9004-3   Guidelines for process materials
ISO 9004-4   Guidelines for quality improvement
ISO 10005   Guidelines for quality plans (prIEC 301-2)
ISO 10007   Guidelines for configuration management (prIEC 301-3)
ISO 10012   Metrological conformation system
ISO 10013   Guideline for quality manuals

require registration to ISO 9000, conformity assessment requires a quality management system. The EU prefers ISO 9000; however, it is not required for most products. It does require that you document your entire manufacturing and quality processes. **Every stage must be documented.** You must have the processes in place to provide the documentation for the TCF. The TCF is your proof of compliance.

The quality system sections in the EU Directives never state that you must have an ISO 9000 (EN 29000) system, except in the *Certification and Technical Standards Directive* (83/189/EEC) and the *Modules of Conformity Assessment Directive* (93/465/EEC). These directives state that you must have a registered quality system. In 83/189/EEC and 93/465/EEC, "registered quality system" is defined as registration to ISO 9000.

Under EU law, being ISO 9000 registered provides a greater amount of liability protection. The Europeans consider registration to ISO 9000 to represent that you have done everything you could do to ensure a quality product. Also, many of your EU customers will expect you to become registered.

Many American manufacturers have made the mistake of assuming that ISO 9000 registration is the same as compliance to the EU Directives. It is

Documentation of the Quality System

Directive	*ISO 9001*
(a) The manufacturer's quality objectives.	**4.1 Management Responsibility** 4.1 Management Responsibilities 4.1.1 Quality Policy 4.2 Quality System
(b) The organization of the business:	**4.12 Organization**
• The organizational structures, the responsibilities of the managerial staff and their organizational authority where quality of design and manufacture of the products is concerned.	4.1 Management Responsibility 4.4 Design Control 4.1.2.1 Responsibilities and Authorizations 4.1.2.2 Resources and Personnel 4.1.2.3 Management Representative
• The methods of monitoring the quality system, especially its ability to achieve the desired quality of design and of the product. It must also include a description of the process used to handle nonconforming products.	4.13 Management Review 4.4 Design Control 4.13 Nonconformity 4.14 Corrective and Preventive Action 4.17 Internal Audits ISO 10007
(c) The procedures for monitoring and verifying the design of the products:	**4.4 Design Control** 4.4.1 General Requirements 4.4.2 Design and Development Planning
• General description of the product, including any changes planned.	4.4.3 Design Inputs 4.4.4 Design Outputs 4.4.5 Design Verification 4.4.9 Design Changes
• The design specifications, including the standards which will be applied and the result of the risks assessment. If you choose not to follow the standards, you must describe how you have met the essential requirements of the directive.	4.4.5 Design Verification 4.5 Document Control 4.6 Purchasing 4.6.4 Verification of Purchased Product 4.6.2 Subcontractors 4.5 Documentation Control 4.4.5 Design Verification
• The techniques used to control and verify the design and the processes and systematic measures which will be used when the products are being designed.	4.3 Contract Review 4.4 Design Control 4.5 Document Control 4.4.5 Design Verification 4.8 Product Identification

Documentation of the Quality System

Directive	*ISO 9001*
	4.15 Handling, Storage, Packaging and Delivery
• The draft label and, where appropriate, instructions for use.	4.8 Product Identification
	4.5 Document and Data Control
• If the device is to be connected to other device(s) in	4.8 Product Identification
order to operate, proof must	4.4.7 Design Verification
be provided that it still conforms to the essential requirements when connected.	4.6.4 Verification of Purchased Product
	4.10 Inspection and Testing
(d) The inspection and quality assurance techniques at the manufacturing stage:	
	4.9 Process Control
	4.10 Inspection and Testing
	4.11 Testing Equipment
	4.12 Inspection and Testing Status Reports
	4.12 Control of Nonconforming Product
	4.13 Corrective Action
	4.17 Internal Audits
	4.18 Training
	4.20 Statistical Techniques
• Identification procedures	ISO Guide 25
drawn up and kept up to	ISO 10012-1
date from drawings, specifications, or other relevant	4.5 Document Control
documents at every stage	4.8 Product Identification and Traceability
of manufacture.	4.9 Process Control
	4.13 Control of Nonconforming Products
(e) The appropriate tests and trials which will be carried out	4.15 Handling, Storage, Packaging and Delivery
before, during, and after manufacture. You must describe the	4.16 Quality Record
	4.2.2 Quality Plan
frequency with which they will	4.3.1 Quality Manual
take place, and the test equipment used. You must be able	4.10 Inspection and Testing
	4.11 Testing Equipment
	4.20 Statistical Techniques
to trace the calibration methods of the test instrument back	4.9 Process Control
	4.16 Quality Records
to a known national standard.	4.17 Internal Audits
	4.19 Service
	4.20 Statistical Techniques

not the same. **ISO 9000 registration is one step in compliance to the EU Directives.**

There is a difference between product compliance and quality system compliance in the EU. ISO 9000 registration may be required for product compliance. Whether or not you have to be registered, you must have a quality system which ensures that your product is manufactured in compliance with the EU Directives. Product compliance is represented by EC Type-Examination. Both are performed by a Notified Body, but they are not the same process. Many manufacturers or service providers assume that if their product meets the testing, then the product is in compliance. In the EU, they anticipate that the product will meet the testing, but want additional assurance that the manufacturing process will always produce the required level of quality. This philosophy forms the basis of the EU compliance system.

When obtaining your registration, you must choose a Notified Body in Europe to audit and certify your ISO quality management system. You cannot choose a registrar that is not an EU Notified Body. Also, you must include the registration process within the conformity assessment procedure for your product or service. ISO 9000 is intertwined with the conformity assessment procedure. If you attempt to do your ISO registration first, you will end up reworking some of the processes to meet the requirements of the directives. **ISO 9000 registration will be based upon your TCF.** It provides the documentation for the ISO audit. ISO 9000 registration and the conformity assessment procedure should be a comprehensive, coordinated effort.

After registration, you must undergo surveillance. You will sign a contract with the Notified Body to conduct surveillance audits for three years. Because your CE Marking is dependent upon your ISO 9000 registration, your CE Marking is only good for three years. Your CE Marking is dependent upon two things: your approved quality management system (ISO 9000) and your EC Type-Examination. While you will have to go through the entire certification procedure again, by maintaining and adding changes to your system as you go along, you should not have to build your conformity assessment system from the ground up. You should only have to make minor updates and repeat the testing. The reregistration process should be much cheaper and easier. The EC product certification may be for a longer time period, so you may not have to repeat this step. However, your CE Marking will still run out.

The failure rate for reregistration in Europe has been running anywhere from 10 to 25%, depending upon the industry. ISO is going to revise EN 29000 to hopefully correct this problem. ISO 9000 standards will be revised in 1999. In the next revision, emphasis will be placed upon:

1. Customer expectations and needs
2. New process guidelines which will ensure that the documentation states that the process was run correctly
3. Clarifying the non-conformity procedures
4. Process feedback documentation
5. Clarifying your monitoring of the quality system
6. Analyzing critical areas of the process and its documentation

These clarifications are supposed to more clearly define the connection between the requirements of the EU Directives and ISO 9000 and reduce the failure rate of reregistration. Until this is complete, there is no substitute for good preparation and management commitment.

In the EU, there are specific harmonized standards which apply ISO 9000 to a specific directive. The ISO 9000 requirements usually stay the same. These standards usually reiterate that the ISO 9000 requirements must be used to reflect the requirements of the individual directives. ISO 9000 is not viewed as a stand-alone process in Europe. An example of this is EN 46001/2, which applies ISO 9000 to medical devices. These standards make the ISO 9000 quality management system into a product standard. So far, not many of these standards have been issued, but over time, almost all major directives will have them.

EOTC is also issuing guidelines for auditors to use when assessing an ISO 9000 quality system. These guidelines are specific to a directive. They are not mandatory, but they are recommended. Many Notified Bodies will expect you to be aware of them. You can obtain these guidelines from your Notified Body or from the Commission.

Politics and the EU

Support for the EU by its citizens depends upon economic conditions. The economic growth from the formation of the EU has not yet resulted in job growth. The EU has been racked by a number of scandals involving the misappropriation of funds, which vindicates the public perception that the EU operates as a closed club. These factors have contributed to the lack of public support. However, the free movement of goods and the common Custom Union will go forward. This phase is too far along to be stopped by national political problems.

The EU has postponed the restructuring and worker reductions that have occurred in the United States, but EU industries are still facing the same problem that led to reengineering in America. The new prosperity brought on by unification has occurred slowly and has not spread uniformly. This is to be expected because the required infrastructure and regulations are just now being completed. In 1997, EU citizens will start to see the benefit of the free movement of goods. EU businesses are already seeing it.

Many countries in the EU are still experiencing the recession from which the United States has only recently recovered. For example, English industry has been slow to modernize. The growth rate throughout the 1990s in England was under 1.5%, which is insufficient to generate the capital required to modernize the economy. This has influenced most English to view the EU as ineffective and restrictive. They have not seen the improvement in the grass roots economy that was promised by the politicians. The English unions are also resisting the changes required to make the industry competitive. Furthermore, modernization always leads to a reduction in the total work force employed at a particular facility, and the only way to avoid this reduction is to expand market share. Expanding market share requires the improved quality and reliability that come from modernization. Regulatory changes can increase the opportunity to expand market share, but modernization and regulatory forces must work together.

On the whole, Europeans find themselves unable to compete in the world marketplace. The formation of the EU has resulted in economic improvements, but the high unemployment rate has masked most of the economic benefits. The economic benefits will probably start to have a positive effect on the EU economy that will be noticeable to the citizens in 1997. Canada has lost 50,000 jobs and the United States has lost 60,000 jobs to the EU. These job losses outside the EU should accelerate in 1997 as the penalties for non-compliance by exporters start to be imposed by the Custom Union. Once opportunities are created, local companies will expand to fill the void. The market share lost by the exporters to the EU will probably be permanent for most companies. Consequently, EU companies will experience growth as they fill the voids left by the out-of-business third-country companies. In areas such as medical devices, most manufacturers in the United States generate 20 to 30% of their total business from exports, with the bulk going to the EU. Without this export market, these companies cannot survive.

The EU free movement of goods will continue. The political and monetary union will occur before the year 2000, but will probably be limited to only a few of the Member States initially. The others, including England, will probably revert back to associate members. Once the economies of these countries improve, the majority will eventually elect full membership. This will only be a transition period, not an end to the EU. In time, all of Europe and the old Soviet satellites will be one economic unit. The Eastern European countries should have less trouble making the transition than some of the Mediterranean countries.

Can American industry respond in time? Since Americans only seem to be able to react to direct threats, some businesses will have to go under before American industry starts to respond. Examples should start appearing by the end of 1996. Many U.S. companies that have responded to the new regulatory climate are increasing their market share in the EU. This increase has been as high as 15%. While the smaller companies are the most likely to fail, the additional resources required to conform to the EU requirements are small, and in most cases companies are already spending the equivalent amount or more to comply with the old regulations. Not only will complying with the EU Directives increase your market share, but it will probably also reduce your current cost of compliance.

Thoughts on the Process of Compliance

The biggest barrier to change is still attitude. It is human nature to want thing to remain the way they are, and the politics of change fosters resistance. Remember that 80% of what you are doing now will not be changed by the new EU compliance requirements. The job of management is to recognize what does not have to be changed and to permit the employees to make the necessary changes. In most cases, it does not matter how something is done as long as the results meet the standards. To successfully implement the new regulatory compliance requirements, you must:

1. Read the required directives and standards and make them readily available to your personnel.
2. Provide the necessary funding and management support.
3. Set up a short time line. This will aid in identifying the management roadblocks that need to be removed or bypassed.
4. Focus on reducing paperwork to only what is necessary. If you do not want to be audited on unnecessary forms, do not use them. When evaluating a form, always ask, "What is the purpose?" and "What is the value of the document?"

5. Use an electronic system; it is cheaper than paper and provides better tracking.
6. Do not talk about training—just do it. In my experience, I have always learned more by teaching a subject. Require personnel to go to a class to share the information and train their co-workers.
7. Remember the Dilbert Principle,* and shorten the work week to 40 hours. This can be done by eliminating the bottlenecks in the decision process. Employees see an immediate benefit, which will reduce the resistance to change.

By reading the directives and understanding the EU compliance process, you can avoid lost market share. The EU compliance system will be the world standard, whether or not you agree. Acting like an ostrich will only make you the loser. You can handle change in two ways: either embrace it as a challenge or reject it as an enemy. The latter method will only put a "for sale" sign on your front door. Japan and the Southeast Asian countries have learned this lesson well. To avoid repeating the history of the automotive, steel, shipbuilding, and textile weaving industries, learn from their mistakes. Realize that no decision is just as bad as a wrong decision, except that it takes much longer to recognize the results. Leveling the playing field will benefit all in the long run.

---

* *The Dilbert Principle: A Cubicle's-Eye View of Bosses, Meetings, Management Fads & Other Workplace Afflictions*, Scott Adams, Harper Business, New York, 1996, p. 315.

Appendix 1:
The Outline for
Harmonization Directive

European Community
COUNCIL RESOLUTION

of 7 May 1985

on a new approach to
technical harmonization and standards

(85/C 136/01)

COUNCIL AND COMMISSION
DECISION OF THE COUNCIL AND THE COMMISSION

of 2 May 1992

on the conclusion of the treaty on the European Economic Area
between the European Commission, their Member States, and the
Republic of Austria, the Republic of Finland, Republic of Iceland, the
Principality of Liechtenstein, the Kingdom of Norway, the Kingdom
of Sweden, and the Swiss Confederation

(92/C 305/66)

THE COUNCIL, *in extension of* its conclusions on standardization, approved on 16 July 1984 (*Annex I*) (p. 2);

emphasizes the urgent need to resolve the present situation as regards technical barriers and dispel the consequent uncertainty for economic operators;

emphasizes the importance and desirability of the new approach which provides for reference to standards—primarily European standards, but national ones if need be, as a transitional measure for the purposes of defining the technical characteristics of products, an approach outlined by the Commission in its communication of 31 January 1985, which follows certain guidelines adopted by the European Parliament in its resolution of 16 October 1980 and forms part of the extension of the Council's conclusions of 16 July 1984;

aware that the new approach will have to be accompanied by a policy on the assessment of conformity, calls on the Commission to give this matter priority and to expedite all its work in this area;

approves the guidelines encapsulated in the list of principles and main elements to be embodied in the main part of the Directives (*Annex II to this resolution*) (p. 3);

calls on the Commission to submit suitable proposals as soon as possible.

ANNEX I

CONCLUSIONS ON STANDARDIZATION
Approved by the Council on 16 July 1984

The Council believes that standardization goes a long way towards ensuring that industrial products can be marketed freely and also towards creating a standard technical environment for undertakings in all countries, which improves competitiveness not only on the Community market but also on external markets, especially in new technology.

It recognizes that the objectives being pursued by the Member States to protect the safety and health of their people as well as the consumer are equally valid in principle, even if different techniques are used to achieve them.

Accordingly, the Council adopts the following principles for a European standardization policy:

- agreement by the Member States to keep a constant check on the technical regulations which are applied—whether *de jure or de facto*—on their territory so as to withdraw those which are obsolete or unnecessary;

- agreement by the Member States to ensure the mutual recognition of the results of tests and the establishment, where necessary, of harmonized rules as regards the operation of certification bodies;

- agreement to early Community consultation at an appropriate level, in accordance with the objectives of Directive [83/189/EEC] where major national regulatory initiatives or procedures might have adverse repercussions on the operation of the internal market;

- extension of the Community practice in matters of technical harmonization of entrusting the task of defining the technical characteristics of products to standards, preferably European but, if necessary, national, where the conditions necessary for this purpose, particularly as regards health protection and safety, are fulfilled;

- a very rapid strengthening of the capacity to standardize, preferably at European level, with a view to facilitating on the one hand harmonization of legislation by the Community and on the other industrial development, particularly in the field of new technologies, since this could in specific circumstances involve the Community in introducing new procedures to improve the drawing up of standards (*e.g.*—standardization bureaus, *ad hoc* committees). The adoption of European standards would be submitted to the European standardization bodies for approval.

In high technology sectors particularly, subjects should be identified where common specifications and standards will make for efficient exploitation of the Community dimension and the opening of public works and supply contracts so that the decisions required in this connection may be taken.

ANNEX II

GUIDELINES FOR A NEW APPROACH TO TECHNICAL HARMONIZATION AND STANDARDS*

The following are the four fundamental principles on which the new approach is based:

- legislative harmonization is limited to the adoption, by means of Directives based on Article 100 of the EEC Treaty, of the essential safety requirements (or other requirements in the general interest) with which products put on the market must conform, and which should therefore enjoy free movement throughout the Community,

- the task of drawing up the technical specifications needed for the production and placing on the market of products conforming to the essential requirements established by the Directives, while taking into account the current stage of technology, is entrusted to organizations competent in the standardization area

- these technical specifications are not mandatory and maintain their status of voluntary standards,

- but, at the same time, national authorities are obliged to recognize that products manufactured in conformity with harmonized standards (or, provisionally, with national standards) are presumed to conform to the 'essential requirements' established by the Directive. (This signifies that the producer has the choice of not manufacturing in conformity with the

---

* OJ No. L 1, 3.1.1994, p. 1. This act was amended by the Treaty.

Article 1

The Agreement on the European Economic Area between the European Communities; their Member States and the Republic of Austria, the Republic of Finland, the Republic of Iceland, the Principality of Liechtenstein, the Kingdom of Sweden, and the Swiss Confederation, the Protocols, the Annexes annexed thereto and the Declarations, the Agreed Minutes and exchanged letters attached to the Final Act are hereby approved on behalf of the European Community and the European Coal and Steel Community.

The tests of the acts referred to in this paragraph are attached to this Decision.

Article 2

The act of approval provided for in Article 129 of the Agreement shall be deposited by the President of the Council on behalf of the European Community and by the President of the Commission on behalf of the European Coal and Steel Community.

standards but that, in this event, he has an obligation to prove that his products conform to the essential requirements of the Directive.)

In order that this system may operate it is necessary:

- on the one hand that the standards offer a guarantee of quality with regard to the 'essential requirements' established by the Directives,

- on the other hand that the public authorities keep intact their responsibility for the protection of safety (or other requirements envisaged) on their territory.

The quality of harmonized standards must be ensured by standardization mandates, conferred by the Commission, the execution of which must conform to the general guidelines which have been the subject of agreement between the Commission and the European standardization organizations. In so far as national standards are concerned, their quality must be verified by a procedure at Community level managed by the Commission, assisted by a standing committee composed of officials from national administrations.

At the same time, safeguard procedures must be provided for, under the management of the Commission assisted by the same committee, in order to allow the competent public authorities the possibility of contesting the conformity of a product, the validity of a certificate or the quality of a standard.

In following this system of legislative harmonization in each area in which it is feasible, the Commission intends to be able to halt the proliferation of excessively technical separate Directives for each product. The scope of Directives according to the 'general reference to standards' formula should encompass wide product categories and types of risk.

The Community could on the one hand, therefore, complete the extremely complex undertaking of harmonizing technical legislation and on the other hand promote the development and application of European standards. These are essential conditions for the improvement of the competitiveness of its industry.

OUTLINE OF THE PRINCIPLES AND MAIN ELEMENTS WHICH SHOULD MAKE UP THE BODY OF THE DIRECTIVES

A. JUSTIFICATIONS

Amongst the traditional principles justifying a Directive the following aspects should be emphasized:

- Member States have the responsibility of ensuring safety on their territory (in the home, at the workplace, etc.) of persons, domestic animals and goods, or the respect of other essential protection requirements in the general interest such as health, consumer or environmental protection etc., with regard to the hazards covered by the Directive itself;*

- the national provisions ensuring such protection must be harmonized in order to ensure the free movement of goods, without lowering existing and justified levels of protection in the Member States;

- CEN and CENELEC (one or the other, or both according to the products covered by the Directive) are the competent bodies to adopt European harmonized standards within the scope of the Directive, in accordance with the guidelines which the Commission, after consultation of the Member States, has signed with these bodies.**

1. In this outline a general approach is developed which should be applied according to the needs for legislation by Directives based on Article 100 of the Treaty relating to sectors or families of products as well as types of hazard.

2. The object of the Directive will be specified in each sphere of application according to the types of hazard (safety, health, environmental, consumer protection, etc.) and should the need arise to the circumstances (in the home, at the place of work, under road traffic conditions, during leisure activities, etc.).

3. Where appropriate, it should be stated that the Member States may make provision, in accordance with Community law, for national regulations concerning the conditions for use of products covered by the scope of the Directive.

4. Concerning the objective mentioned in the second principle, it is obvious that it is carried into effect by the very adoption of the Directive under Article 100 of the Treaty, as the essential safety requirements contained in it are of such a nature as to ensure the pursuit of such an objective.

---

* For reasons of convenience and ease of drafting, the rest of this document refers only to safety.

** For specific sectors of industrial activity, other competent European bodies for the drawing up of technical specifications could be involved.

B. MAIN ELEMENTS

I. Scope
Definition of the range of products covered, as well as the nature of the hazards it is intended to avert.

The scope should be defined in such a way that a consistent approach to the action is ensured, and that the proliferation of Directives on specific products is avoided. Besides, it should be noted that the enacting terms of such a Directive do not preclude the possibility of several Directives being adopted on one and the same product according to the various types of hazard associated with that product (for example, mechanical safety of a machine on the one hand and pollution by that machine on the other hand).

II. General clause for placing on the market
The products covered by the Directive may be placed on the market only if they do not endanger the safety of persons, domestic animals or goods when properly installed and maintained and used for the purposes for which they are intended.

1. The Directives would provide for total harmonization as a general rule. Consequently, any product placed on the market falling within the scope of the Directive must be in conformity with the requirements of the Directive. In certain specific conditions, optional harmonization for certain products may prove to be opportune. The outline Directive, however, is drawn up with a view to total harmonization.

   Appropriate solutions could be envisaged in order to take account of the need to support, in some Member States, a harmonious move towards the introduction of a system of binding regulations, in order in particular to ensure the establishment of appropriate certification infra-structures.

   Point II therefore represents a general clause setting out the responsibilities of the Member States in relation to the placing of goods on the market.

2. In order to respect the general principle on which the outline Directive is based, which is to leave to the trade the choice of the means of attestation of conformity and thus to prohibit Member States from setting up any system of control prior to placing on the market (except, of course, in cases where prior control is required by specific Directives for special sectors, as is besides clearly provided for in *point VIII* [p. 11]), it is obvious that the national authorities in order to acquit themselves

of their responsibilities set out in this clause must be allowed to exercise control on the market by way of spot checks.

3. In certain cases, in particular with regard to the protection of workers and consumers, the conditions set out in this clause may be strengthened (foreseeable use).

III. Essential safety requirements

Description of the safety requirements which are essential for the application of the general clause in *point II* (p. 5–6) with which all products covered by the Directive must conform.

1. The essential safety requirements which must be met in the case of products which can be put on the market shall be worded precisely enough in order to create, on transposition into national law, legally binding obligations which can be enforced. They should be so formulated as to enable the certification bodies straight away to certify products as being in conformity, having regard to those requirements in the absence of standards. The degree of detail of the wording will depend on the subject matter. If the basic requirements for safety are observed, the general clause in *point II* can be applied.

2. Amendments to these requirements can be made only by means of a new Council Directive under Article 100 of the Treaty.

IV. Free movement clause

Obligation on the Member States to accept, under the conditions referred to in point V, the free movement of products which conform to *points II and III* (p. 5–7) .

1. Free movement will be ensured in the case of products declared to conform to the protection requirements laid down in the Directive, without recourse as a general rule to prior verification of compliance with the requirements set out in *point III*, it being understood that *note 2* of *point II* (p. 6) also applies in this case.

   The interpretation to be given to this provision should not have the consequence that third party certification is to be systematically required by the sectoral Directives.

2. The actual aim of the Directives in question is to cover all essential requirements, but in the exceptional case of cover proving incomplete,

it would always be possible for a Member State to act under Article 36 of the Treaty.

V. Means of proof of conformity and effects

1. Member States shall presume to be in conformity with *points II and III* (p. 5–6) products which are accompanied by one of the means of attestation described in *point VIII* (p. 11) declaring that they are in conformity with:

   (a) the harmonized standards adopted by the European standardization body which is particularly competent within the scope of this Directive, when these standards are adopted in accordance with the general guidelines agreed between that body and the Commission and the references of which are published in the *Official Journal of the European Communities*; such publication should, besides, also be carried out by the Member States;

   (b) or as a transitional measure, and in so far as harmonized standards do not exist in the field covered by such standards, national standards referred to in *paragraph 2.*

2. Member States shall communicate to the Commission the text of those national standards which they consider to meet *points II and III*. The Commission shall forthwith forward this text to the other Member States. In accordance with the procedure laid down in *paragraph 2 of Point VI* (p. 9), the Commission shall notify the Member States of the national standards which enjoy the presumption of conformity with *points II and III*.

   Member States are required to publish the references of these standards. The Commission shall also ensure that they are published in the *Official Journal of the European Communities.*

3. Member States shall accept that the products for which the manufacturer has not applied any standard (because of absence of a standard as laid down in *paragraphs I (a) and (b)* above or for other exceptional reasons) are considered to be in conformity with *points II and III* (p. 5–6), when their conformity is demonstrated by one of the means of attestation set out in *point VIII, paragraph I (a) and (b)* (p. 11).

   1. Only those means of attestation provided for in *point VIII* (p. 11) necessarily carry presumption of conformity.

   2. The presumption of conformity is constituted by the fact that the conformity of a product to harmonized or national standards is declared by

one of the means of attestation set out in *point VIII*. When the product is not in conformity with a standard, because the standards do not exist or because the manufacturer, for example in cases of innovation, prefers to apply other manufacturing criteria of his choice, conformity to *points II and III* is declared by the means of an attestation delivered by an independent body.

3. In cases under *point V, paragraphs I and 3* (p. 7–8), Member States will therefore have the right, for the presumption to operate, to request at any time one of the means of attestation set out in *point VIII*.

4. The drafting and adoption of the harmonized standards mentioned in *paragraph I (a)* by the **CEN** and **CENELEC**, these bodies being generally considered to be the 'European standards bodies which are particularly competent', and the obligation relating to transposition into national standards are governed by these two bodies' internal rules and their regulations relating to standards work. The internal rules of **CEN** and **CENELEC** are in the process of being harmonized. However, it is not ruled out that the harmonized standards referred to in *paragraph I (a)* will be prepared outside **CEN** and **CENELEC** by other bodies which may assume these functions in particular areas; in such cases adoption of the harmonized standards shall be submitted for approval by **CEN/CENELEC**. In any case, the drafting and introduction of the harmonized standards referred to in *point V* (p. 7–8) must be subject to the guidelines agreed between the Commission and these organizations. The guidelines deal in particular with the following principles and conditions:

- the availability of suitable staff and technical infrastructure at the standards body which the Commission mandates to proceed with standardization;

- the association of public authorities and interested circles (in particular manufacturers, users, consumers, unions);

- the adoption of harmonized standards and their transposition into national standards or, at least, the annulment of diverging national standards under conditions approved by the Commission when drawing up a frame of reference for standardization after consultation with the Member States.

5. In the selection of national standards, due consideration will be given to any practical difficulties arising from that selection.

National standards are selected only on a transitional basis. Accordingly, when a selection decision is made, the relevant European bodies will in principle be sent instructions to draft and adopt the corresponding 'European standards' within a given period of time and under the conditions stated above.

VI. Management of the list of standards

1. Where a Member State or the Commission considers that harmonized standards or drafts thereof do not fully satisfy *points II and III* (p. 56), the Commission or the Member State shall bring this to the attention of the committee *(point X)* (p. 13) setting out the reasons. The committee shall give an opinion as a matter of urgency.

   The Commission shall, in the light of the committee's opinion, notify the Member States of the necessity of withdrawing or not withdrawing the standard from the publication referred to in *point V, paragraph 1 (a)* (p. 7). It shall inform the European standards body concerned and, if necessary, give it a new or revised mandate.

2. On receipt of the communication referred to in *point V, paragraph 2* (p. 8), the Commission shall consult the committee. After the committee has given its opinion, the Commission shall, within a given period, notify the Member States whether the national standard in question should or should not enjoy presumption of conformity and, if so, be subject to national publication of its references.

   If the Commission or a Member State considers that a national standard no longer fulfills the conditions for presumption of conformity to the safety requirements, the Commission shall consult the committee. In the light of the opinion of the committee, it shall notify the Member States whether or not the standard in question should continue to enjoy presumption of conformity and in the latter case be withdrawn from the publications referred to in *point V, paragraph 2*.

   As indicated above (see notes to *point V, paragraph 2*), the Member States have the power to decide which of their national standards may be considered to be in conformity with *points I and III* (p. 5–6) and thus be subject to the Commission confirmation procedure.

VII. Safeguard clause

1. Where a Member State finds that a product might compromise the safety of individuals, domestic animals or property, it shall take all appropriate mea-

sures to withdraw or prohibit the placing on the market of the product in question or to restrict its free movement even if it is accompanied by one of the means of attestation referred to in *point VIII* (p. 11).

Within a given period of time, and only when the product in question is accompanied by one of the means of attestation provided for in *point VIII*, the Member State shall inform the Commission of such a measure. It will indicate the reasons for its decision and in particular whether the non-conformity results from:

(a) non-compliance with *points II and III* (p. 5–6) (when the product does not conform to any standard);

(b) incorrect application of the standards referred to in *point V* (p. 7–9);

(c) a shortcoming in the standards themselves.

2. The Commission shall consult the Member States concerned as soon as possible. If the Member State which has taken measures intends to maintain them, the Commission shall refer the matter to the committee within a specified period. Where the Commission, after consultation of the committee, finds that the action is justified it shall, also within a given period of time, inform the Member State in question and point out to the other Member States that (all else being equal) they are also obliged to prevent the product in question from being placed on the market.

3. Where failure of the product to comply with *points II and III* (p. 5–6) results from a shortcoming in the harmonized standards or in the national standards, the consequences shall be those set out in *point VI* (p. 9–10).

4. Where the non-conforming product is accompanied by a means of attestation issued by an independent body or by the manufacturer, the competent Member State shall take the appropriate measures against the author of the attestation and inform the Commission and the other Member States.

5. The Commission shall ensure that all Member States are kept informed of the progress and of the outcome of this procedure.

This point describes the consequences when recourse by a Member State to the safeguard clause appears to be justified. It does not give any indication on the consequences when recourse does not appear to be justified after expiry of the Community examination procedure, because in such cases the general rules of the Treaty apply.

VIII. Means of attestation of conformity

1. The means of attestation referred to in *point V* (p. 7–9) which the trade may use are:

   (a) certificates and marks of conformity issued by a third party;

   (b) results of tests carried out by a third party;

   (c) declaration of conformity issued by the manufacturer or his agent based in the Community. This may be coupled with the requirement for a surveillance system;

   (d) other means of attestation which could possibly be determined in the Directive.

2. The choice by trade and industry between these different means may be limited, or even removed, according to the nature of the products and hazards covered by the Directive.

3. National bodies authorized to issue marks or certificates of conformity shall be notified by each Member State to the Commission and to the other Member States.

   1. The appropriate means of attestation will be established and expanded in the specific Directives taking into account the special requirements of their scope. It must be borne in mind that the certification bodies designated by the Member States for *cases (a) and (b)* will have to intervene in particular in the absence of standards and where the manufacturer does not observe standards (*see point V, paragraph 3* [p. 8]).

   2. The bodies referred to in *paragraph 3* must carry out their duties according to recognized international practices and principles and especially in accordance with **ISO Guides.** The responsibility for the control of the operation of these bodies lies with the Member States. Questions concerning the carrying out of tests and certification may be put before the committee set up under *point IX* (p. 13).

   3. With regard to the manufacturer's declaration of conformity, the national authorities have the right to ask the manufacturer or the importer to communicate the data relating to the tests carried out concerning safety etc., when they have good grounds for believing that a product does not offer the degree of safety required in all respects. Refusal on the part of the manufacturer or the importer to communicate these data constitutes sufficient reason to doubt the presumption of conformity.

4. The determination of a limitative list of means of attestation only concerns the system of presumption of conformity but cannot have the effect of restricting the possibility for a member of the trade to prove, by any means he sees fit within the framework of a dispute or court proceedings, the conformity of the product with *points II and III* (p. 5–6).

IX. Standing committee

A standing committee shall be set up chaired by a representative of the Commission and consisting of representatives appointed by the Member States who may avail themselves of the help of experts or advisers.

The committee shall be convened by its chairman either on his own initiative or at the request of a Member State.

The committee shall draw up its own rules of procedure.

X. Tasks and operation of the committee

1. The committee shall carry out the tasks entrusted to it by virtue of the foregoing points.

2. Furthermore, any question regarding the implementation of a Directive may be submitted to the committee.

The tasks of the committee shall be concerned with the implementation of the Directive. The object of the consultation of the Committee prior to the publication of the references of the national standards is more to provide for a forum for the discussion of the objections which the Commission or a Member State may formulate, than to carry out a systematic examination of the entire contents of the standards.

Criteria for choosing the priority areas in which this approach could initially be applied

1. The need to find a new approach to the harmonization of technical regulations, based on 'general reference to standards' and following the lines described earlier, is the outcome of a number of conditions (outlined in the first part of this communication) backed up by the experience already acquired by the Community. Consequently it is a general principle, the validity of which will have to be assessed in practical terms in the various areas in which it will be applied.

The Council took a similar view in its 'Conclusions' of 16 July 1984 when it confirmed the general need for an extension of the 'general reference to standards' practice, but only provided the necessary conditions were fulfilled (*i.e.*—as regards the obligation on public authorities to protect the health and safety of their citizens).

2. Before the priority areas in which this approach should initially be applied can be chosen, it is therefore necessary to establish a number of selection criteria to be taken into consideration, criteria which cannot taken separately.

   (a) Since the approach calls for the 'essential requirements' to be harmonized and made mandatory by Directives based on Article 100 of the Treaty, the 'general reference to standards' approach will be appropriate only where it is genuinely possible to distinguish between 'essential requirements' and 'manufacturing specifications'. In other words, in all areas in which the essential requirements in the public interest are such that a large number of manufacturing specifications have to be included if the public authorities are to keep intact their responsibility for protection of their citizens, the conditions for the 'general reference to standards' approach are not fulfilled as this approach would have little sense. In the light of this statement areas involving safety protection certainly appear to have priority over those involving health protection (which applies to the scope of Directive [83/189/EEC]).

   (b) If 'general reference to standards' is to be possible, the area concerned must be covered by, or be capable of being covered by, standardization. Areas which are inherently ill suited to standardization work are certainly the areas referred to in (a) above where the need for regulations is felt unanimously throughout the Community. In other areas there is a standardization capacity or potential and in the latter case the Community should encourage it in close cooperation with both the industry concerned and the European standards bodies, whilst ensuring that the interests of consumers are taken into account.

   (c) The progress of technical harmonization work in the Community under the general [program] established by the Council resolutions of 1969 and 1973 varies greatly from one industrial sector to another. In manufacturing industry (which appears at first sight better to fulfill the abovementioned criteria) most of the Directives adopted concern three areas: motor vehicles, metrology and electrical equipment.

The new approach will therefore have to take this state of affairs into account and concentrate mainly on other areas in which there is a lack of Community activities (*e.g.*—many engineering products and building materials) without calling into question regulations that are already well advanced (for example those referring to motor vehicles). The case of electrical equipment is different: this is the only area to have been tackled by a Directive of the 'general reference to standards' type and should certainly be included in the priority areas for all such products not yet covered, in view of the extremely important part played in this area by international and European standardization.

(d) One of the main purposes of the new approach is to make it possible to settle at a stroke, with the adoption of a single Directive, all the problems concerning regulations for a very large number of products, without the need for frequent amendments or adaptations to that Directive. Consequently, in the selected areas, there should be a wide range of products sufficiently homogeneous to allow common 'essential requirements' to be defined. This general criterion is, however, based mainly on practical and [labor-saving] considerations. There is nothing to prevent a single type of product, in certain cases, from being covered by the 'general reference to standards' formula if all the abovementioned criteria are met.

(e) Finally, mention should be made of one criterion that the Commission, in agreement with industry, has always regarded as essential. There must be grounds for considering that the existence of different regulations does in practice genuinely impede the free movement of goods. In some cases, however, even if these grounds are not obvious, a Directive may appear necessary to protect an essential public interest uniformly throughout the Community.

Appendix 2:
Product Liability Directive

By Brian P. Kujawa

INTRODUCTION*

Before discussing the EU's *Product Liability Directive* (85/374/EEC), it is important to clarify the difference between *regulations* and *directives* in terms of their scope and enactment. While the two are forms of legislation that affect the Member States and how third countries are treated in the area covered,

- **Regulations** are acts of the Council and the European Parliament that affect the Union uniformly. They spell out the means by which they are enacted and enforced. They go into effect on the date specified and affect all the Member States accordingly.
- **Directives**, however, set minimum standards which are to be enacted in the laws, statutes, etc. of the individual Member States. The means by which directives are enacted is up to the Member States *subject to these minimums*.

---

* Disclaimer: This introduction has been prepared from several resource materials by a researcher who, while specializing in the area of law and legal issues, is not an attorney-at-law. Please remember that this is merely resource material. You should consult an attorney if you need advice on pursuing/defending product liability litigation.

On this point, the most common area for litigation by the Commission against a Member State is for failure to enact a directive by the date specified. For example, on January 13, 1993, the EU's Court of Justice found the French government guilty of failing to communicate its laws, regulations, and administrative acts enacting Directive 85/374/EEC (Case C–293/91, ECR I [1993], reported in the *Reports of the European Court of Justice and Courts of First Instance,* No. 01/93, p. 3).

How has the fact that product liability is covered by a directive instead of a regulation affected this area of law? Let's look at a typical product liability case.

Manufacturer A, located in the United States, produces widgets which are put into circulation in the EU by Distributor B via Importer C. Consumer X purchases a widget. In the course of proper use of the widget, his spouse, Y, is seriously injured.

During the course of preparing the personal injury suit, X and Y's attorney discovers that the widget's failure was caused by a faulty component supplied to Manufacturer A by Company D, which is based in the EU. Thus, Consumer X's attorney files suit against A, B, C, and D for:

1. Personal injury of Y
2. Y's pain and suffering
3. Loss of consortium to X
4. Punitive damages as deemed just and proper

Provided that X's attorney files suit within the three-year period of limitations under Article 10, which commences "from the day on which the plaintiff became aware, or should have reasonably become aware of the damage, the defect and the identity of the producer," what are X and Y guaranteed under Directive 85/374/EEC?

1. If the jury finds for Plaintiffs X and Y, Y is entitled to receive compensatory damages.
2. Under Article 5, when there are two or more defendants, each potential defendant is "liable jointly and separately, without prejudice to the provisions of national law concerning the rights of contribution or recourse."

This means that *each* defendant who is successfully sued is liable for the total of the damages awarded regardless of the degree that each was responsible for the damage.

Thus, if the jury found for Plaintiff X and awarded $5 million in damages, Defendants A, B, C, and D would *each* be responsible for the entire sum awarded to X. In other words, the jury, when awarding damages, determines the entire sum and does not have to determine "comparative negligence" (i.e., what percent of the sum each defendant is responsible for).

3. Suppose that Manufacturer A's widgets are seriously injuring spouses due to the defective component from Company D all over the EU. Under Article 16(1), all Y's who are so injured or killed would, upon a successful judgment, be entitled to damages totaling at least *70 million ECU* (approximately $90 million as of this writing).

Beyond this, everything else in the product liability area is in accordance with the tort and civil practice laws of each Member State. In "Difficulties Relating to Directives Affecting the Recoverability of Damages for Personal Injuries,"* Andrew Geddes discusses the problems raised in the automobile accident and product liability areas, including:

1. *When does the ten-year absolute period of limitations under Article 11 commence?* According to Article 11, it is left to the Member States to define when "the producer put into circulation the actual product that caused damage." For example, under the Belgian Law on Product Liability of February 25, 1991, this happens upon "the first action by which a producer gives effect to his intentions in regard of his product either by transferring it to a third party or by using it for the benefit of the same."**

   This provides a manufacturer with the following affirmative defense: that he did not put the product in question into circulation.** In our sample case, if A can prove that he did not put the widget into circulation, he should be found not guilty by the jury.

2. Damages beyond compensatory damages (e.g., punitive damages, pain and suffering, loss of consortium, loss of expectation of life, moral damages, biological damages).***

---

* *European Law Review,* vol. 18 (1992), pp. 408, 416–419.

** *Belgisch Staatsblad/Moniteur Belge,* March 22, 1991, p. 5884. As cited in the *European Law Review,* vol. 18 (1992), p. 450.

*** Geddes, p. 417.

3. Jurisdiction (in what Member State(s) the particular cause of action can be tried) and "longarm jurisdiction" (suing non-resident defendants/ defendants not domiciled in the plaintiff's state).

4. In the matter of wrongful death suits, who are defined as the deceased's dependents?

5. In the matter of class action cases arising out of Article 16(1), is there a maximum amount of damages for which plaintiffs can sue a producer? As previously stated, in successful litigation under Article 16(1), plaintiffs are entitled to a minimum of 70 million ECU. However, three Member States (Germany, Greece, and Portugal) have set a ceiling on the amount of damages available.*

6. The ability of a plaintiff to recover the awarded damages once all appeals have been exhausted by the Defendant.** As in the United States, it is possible for a defendant to declare bankruptcy as the result of successful litigation to delay and, if liquidated, avoid paying damages to the plaintiff or creditors. Whether or not a plaintiff can successfully recover will depend on the lien laws of the Member State where the case was heard as well as the bankruptcy laws of the state/nation where the defendant is located.

7. Are defendant producers required to carry liability insurance?***

Thus, in our example, assuming that the jury found for Plaintiffs X and Y, they would only be guaranteed the right to collect the compensatory damages for Y's injury. The remaining damages are at the discretion of the jury and judge in accordance with the laws of the Member State where the case is tried.

As for recovering the damages awarded, if the defendants are forced to declare bankruptcy, X and Y might never see a single dollar of the damages awarded.

Additional Reading

Geddes, Andrew. "Difficulties Relating to Directives Affecting the Recoverability of Damages for Personal Injury." *European Law Review,* vol. 18 (1992), pp. 408–419.

Kelly, P. and Atree, R. (eds.). *European Product Liability,* Butterworths, London, 1992.

McIntosh, David and Holmes, Marjorie. *Personal Injury Awards in the E.C. Countries,* Lloyds of London Press, London, 1991.

---

* Geddes, p. 418.
** Geddes, pp. 418–419.
*** Geddes, p. 419.

COUNCIL DIRECTIVE

of 25 July 1985

on the approximation of the laws, regulations and administrative provisions of the Member States concerning liability for defective products

(85/374/EEC)
[OJ No. L 210, 7.8.1985, p. 29–33]

The Council of the European Communities

Having regard to the Treaty establishing the European Economic Community, and in particular Article 100 thereof,

Having regard to the proposal from the Commission,*

Having regard to the opinion of the European Parliament,**

Having regard to the opinion of the Economic and Social Committee,***

Whereas approximation of the laws of the Member States concerning the liability of the producer for damage caused by the defectiveness of his products is necessary because the existing divergences may distort competition and affect the movement of goods within the Common Market and entail a differing degree of protection of the consumer against damage caused by a defective product to his health or property;

Whereas liability without fault on the part of the producer is the sole means of adequately solving the problem, peculiar to our age of increasing technicality, of a fair apportionment of the risks inherent in modern technological production;

Whereas liability without fault should apply only to [movables] which have been industrially produced; whereas, as a result, it is appropriate to exclude liability for agricultural products and game, except where they have undergone a processing of an industrial nature which could cause a defect in these products; whereas the liability provided for in this Directive should also apply to movables or are installed in inmovables;

---

* OJ No. C 241, 14.10.1976, p. 9 and OJ No. C 271, 26.10.1979, p. 3.
** OJ No. C 127, 21.5.1979, p. 61.
*** OJ No. C 114, 7.5.1979, p. 15.

Whereas protection of the consumer requires that all producers involved in the production process should be made liable, in so far as their finished product, component part or any raw material supplied by them was defective; whereas, for the same reason, liability should extend to importers of products into the Community and to persons who present themselves as producers by affixing their trade name, trade mark or other distinguishing feature or who supply a product the producer of which cannot be identified;

Whereas in situations where several persons are liable for the same damage, the protection of the consumer requires that the injured person should be able to claim full compensation for the damage from anyone of them;

Whereas, to protect the physical well-being and property of the consumer, the defectiveness of the product should be determined by reference **not** to the *fitness for use* **but** to the *lack of safety* which the public at large is entitled to expect; whereas the safety in assessed by excluding any misuse of the product not reasonable under the circumstances [*emphasis added*];

Whereas a fair apportionment of risk between the injured person and the producer implies that the producer should be able to free himself from liability if he furnishes proof as to the existence of certain exonerating circumstances;

Whereas the protection of the consumer requires that the liability of the producer remains unaffected by acts or omission of other persons having contributed to cause the damage; whereas, however, the contributory negligence of the injured person may be taken into account to reduce or disallow such liability;

Whereas the protection of the consumer requires compensation for death and personal injury as well as compensation for damage to property; whereas the latter should nevertheless be limited to goods for private use or consumption and be subject to a deduction of a lower threshold of a fixed amount in order to avoid litigation in an excessive number of cases; whereas this Directive should not prejudice compensation for pain and suffering and other non-material damage payable, where appropriate, under the law applicable to the case;

Whereas a uniform period of limitation for the bringing of action for compensation is in the interests both of the injured and of the producer;

Whereas product age in the course of time, higher safety standards are developed and the state of science and technology progresses; whereas, therefore, it would be reasonable to make the producer liable for an unlimited period for the defectiveness of his product; whereas, therefore, liability should expire after a reasonable length, without prejudice to claims pending at law;

Whereas, to achieve effective protection of consumers, no contractual derogation should be permitted as regards the liability of the producer in relation to the injured person;

Whereas under the legal systems of the Member States an injured party may have a claim for damages based on grounds of contractual liability or on grounds of non-contractual liability other than that provided for in this Directive; in so far as these provisions also serve to attain the objective of effective protection of consumers, they should remain unaffected by this Directive; whereas, in so far as effective protection of consumers in the sector of pharmaceutical products is already attained by the Member States under a special liability system, claims based on this system should similarly remain possible;

Whereas, to the extent that liability for nuclear injury or damage is already covered in all Member States by adequate special rules, it has been possible to exclude damage of this type from the scope of this Directive;

Whereas, since the exclusion of primary agricultural products and game from the scope of this Directive may be felt, in certain Member States, in view of what is expected for the protection of consumers, to restrict unduly such protection, it should be possible for a Member State to extend liability to such products;

Whereas, for similar reasons, the possibility offered to a producer to free himself from liability if he proves that the state of scientific and technical knowledge at the time when he put the product into circulation was not such as to enable the existence of a defect to be discovered may be felt in certain Member States to restrict unduly the protection of the consumer; whereas it should therefore be possible for a Member State to maintain its legislation or to provide by new legislation that this exonerating circumstance is not admitted; whereas, in the case of new legislation, making use of this derogation should, however, be subject to a Community stand-still procedure, in order to raise, if possible, the level of protection in a uniform manner throughout the Community;

Whereas, taking into account the legal traditions in most of the Member States, it is inappropriate to set out any financial ceiling on the producer's liability without fault; whereas, in so far as there are, however, differing traditions, it seems possible to admit that a Member State may derogate from the principle of *unlimited liability* by providing a limit for the total liability of the product for damage resulting from a death or personal injury and caused by identical items with the same defect, provided that this limit is established at a level sufficiently high to guarantee adequate protection of the consumer and the correct functioning of the Common Market;

Whereas the harmonization resulting from this cannot be total at the present stage, but opens the way towards greater harmonization; whereas it is therefore necessary that the Council receive at regular intervals, reports from the Commission on the application of this Directive, accompanied, as the case may be, by appropriate proposals;

Whereas it is particularly important in this respect that a re-examination be carried out of those parts of the Directive relating to the derogation open to the Member States, at the expiry of a period of sufficient length to gather practical experience of the effects of these derogations on the consumers and on the functioning Common Market;

HAS ADOPTED THIS DIRECTIVE:

ARTICLE 1

The producer shall be liable for damage caused by a defect in his product.

ARTICLE 2

For the purposes of this Directive, '**product**' means all movables, with the exception of primary agricultural products and game, even though incorporated into another movable or into an immovable. '**Primary agricultural product**' means the products of the soil, of stock-farming and of fisheries, excluding products which have undergone initial processing. '**Product**' includes electricity.

ARTICLE 3

1. '**Producer**' means the manufacturer of a finished product, the producer of any raw material or the manufacturer of a component part and any person who, by putting his name, trade mark or other distinguishing feature on the product presents himself as its producer.

2. Without prejudice to the liability of the producer, any person who imports into the Community a product for sale, leasing or any form of distribution in the course of his business shall be deemed to be a producer within the meaning of this Directive and shall be responsible as a producer.

3. Where the producer of the product cannot be identified, each supplier of the product shall be treated as its producer unless he informs the injured person,

within a reasonable period of time, of the identity of the producer or of the person who supplied him with the product. The same shall apply, in the case of an imported product, if this product does not indicate the identity of the importer referred to in **paragraph 2**, even if the name of the producer is indicated.

ARTICLE 4

The injured person shall be required to prove the damage, the defect and the causal relationship between the defect and damage.

ARTICLE 5

Where, as a result of the provisions of this Directive, *two or more persons* are liable for the same damage, *they shall be* **liable jointly and separately,** without prejudice to the provisions of national law concerning the rights of *contribution* or *recourse* [*emphasis added*].

ARTICLE 6

1. A product is defective when it does not provide the safety which a person is entitled to expect, taking all circumstances into account, including:

   (a) the presentation of the product;
   (b) the use to which it could reasonably be expected that the product would be put;
   (c) the time when the product was put into circulation.

2. A product shall not be considered defective for the sole reason that a better product is subsequently put into circulation.

ARTICLE 7

The producer shall not be liable as a result of this Directive if he proves:

   (a) that he did not put the product into circulation; or
   (b) that, having regard to the circumstances, it is probable that the defect which caused the damage did not exist at the time when the product was put into circulation by him or that the defect came into being afterwards; or
   (c) that the product was neither manufactured by him for sale or any form of distribution for economic purpose nor manufactured or distributed by him in the course of his business; or

(d) that the defect is due to compliance of the product with mandatory regulations issued by the public authorities; or

(e) that the state of scientific and technical knowledge at the time when he put the product into circulation was not such as to enable the existence of the defect to be discovered; or

(f) in the case of a manufacturer of a component, that the defect is attributable to the design of the product in which the component has been fitted or to the instructions given by the manufacturer of the product.

ARTICLE 8

1. Without prejudice to the provisions of national law concerning the right of contribution or recourse, the liability of the producer shall not be reduced when the damage is caused both by a defect and by the act or omission of a third party.

2. The liability of the producer may be reduced or disallowed when, having regard to all the circumstances, the damage is caused by both a defect in the product and by the fault of the injured person or any person for whom the injured person is responsible.

ARTICLE 9

For the purpose of **Article 1**, '**damage**' means:

(a) damage caused by death or personal injury;

(b) damage to, or destruction of, any item of property other than the defective product itself, with a lower threshold of 500 ECU, provided that the item of property:

   (i) is of a type ordinarily intended for private use or consumption, **and**

   (ii) was used by the injured person mainly for his own private use or consumption.

This Article shall be without prejudice to national provisions relating to non-material damage.

ARTICLE 10

1. Member States shall provide in their legislation that a limitation period of three years shall apply to proceedings for the recovery of damages as provided for in this Directive. The limitation period shall begin to run from the day on

which the plaintiff became aware, or should have reasonably become aware of the damage, the defect and the identity of the producer.

2. The laws of the Member States regulating suspension or interruption of the limitation period shall not be affected by this Directive.

ARTICLE 11

Member States shall provide in their legislation that the rights conferred upon the injured person pursuant to this Directive shall be extinguished upon a period of *10 YEARS* from the date on which the producer put into circulation the actual product which caused the damage, unless the injured person has in the meantime instituted proceedings against the producer.

ARTICLE 12

The liability of the producer arising from this Directive may not, in relation to the injured person, be limited or excluded by a provision limiting his liability or exempting him from liability.

ARTICLE 13

This Directive shall not affect any rights which an injured person may have according to the rules of the law of contractual or non-contractual liability or a special liability system existing at the moment when this Directive is notified.

ARTICLE 14

This Directive shall not apply to injury or damage arising from nuclear accidents and covered by international conventions ratified by the Member States.

ARTICLE 15

1. Each Member State may:

   (a) by way of derogation from **Article 2**, provide in its legislation that within the meaning of **Article 1** of this Directive, '*product*' also means primary agricultural products and game;
   (b) by way of derogation from **Article 7 (e)**, maintain or, subject to the procedure set out in *paragraph 2* of this Article, provide in this legislation that the producer shall be liable even if he proves that the state of scientific and technical knowledge at the time when he put the prod-

uct into circulation was not such as to enable the existence of a defect to be discovered.

2. A Member State wishing to introduce the measure specified in *paragraph 1 (b)* shall communicate the text of the proposed measure to the Commission. The Commission shall inform the other Member States thereof.

The Member State concerned shall hold the proposed measure in abeyance for nine months after the Commission is informed and provided that in the meantime the Commission has not submitted to the Council a proposal amending this Directive on the relevant matter. However, if within *three months* of receiving said information, the Commission does not advise the Member State concerned that it intends submitting such a proposal to the Council, the Member State may take the proposed measure immediately [*emphasis added*].

If the Commission does submit to the Council such a proposal amending this Directive within the aforementioned nine months, the Member State concerned shall hold the proposed measure in abeyance for a further period of *18 months* from the date on which the proposal is submitted [*emphasis added*].

3. Ten years after the date of notification of this Directive, the Commission shall submit to the Council a report on the effect that rulings by the courts as to the application of **Article 7 (e)** and of *paragraph 1 (b)* of this Article have on consumer protection and the functioning of the Common Market. In light of this report, the Council, acting on a proposal from the Commission and pursuant to the terms of Article 100 of the Treaty, shall decide whether to repeal **Article 7 (e)**.

ARTICLE 16

1. Any Member State may provide that a producer's total liability for damage resulting from a death or personal injury and caused by identical items with the same defect shall be limited to an amount which may not be less than **70 million ECU.**

2. Ten years after the date of notification of this Directive, the Commission shall submit to the Council a report on the effect on consumer protection and the functioning of the Common Market of the implementation of the financial limit on liability by those Member States which have used the option provided for in *paragraph 1*. In the light of this report, the Council, acting on a proposal from the Commission and pursuant to Article 100 of the Treaty, shall decide whether to repeal *paragraph 1*.

ARTICLE 17

This Directive shall not apply to products put into circulation before the date on which the provisions referred to in **Article 19** enter into force.

ARTICLE 18

1. For the purposes of this Directive, the **ECU** shall be that defined by **Regulation (EEC) No. 3180/78*** as amended by **Regulation (EEC) No. 2626/84**.** The equivalent in national currency shall initially be calculated at the rate obtaining on the date of adoption of this Directive.

2. Every five years, the Council, acting on a proposal from the Commission, shall examine and, if need be, revise the amounts in this Directive, in light of economic and monetary trends in the Community.

ARTICLE 19

1. Member States shall bring into force, not later than three years from the date of notification of this Directive, the laws, regulations and administrative provisions necessary to comply with this Directive. They shall forthwith inform the Commission thereof.***

2. The procedure set out in **Article 15 (2)** shall apply from the date of notification of this Directive.

ARTICLE 20

Member States shall communicate to the Commission the texts of the main provisions of national law which they subsequently adopt in the field governed by this Directive.

ARTICLE 21

Every five years, the Commission shall present a report to the Council on the application of this Directive and, if necessary, shall submit appropriate proposals to it.

---

* OJ No. L 379, 30.12.1978, p. 1
** OJ No. L 247, 16.9.1984, p. 1.
*** This directive was notified to the Member States on 30 July 1985.

ARTICLE 22

This Directive is addressed to the Member States.
Done at Brussels, 25 July 1985.

For the Council

The President

J. POOS

Appendix 3: Resources

Information

Automotive

AI (Automotive Industries)
2600 Fisher Building, West Grand Blvd., Detroit, MI 48202
Phone: 313-875-2090, fax: 313-875-8148
Free subscription. Covers the automotive industry. Deals with all phases of the industry. Frequent articles on quality and standards.

Auto World
3000 Town Center, Suite 2750, Southfield, MI 48075
Phone: 800-441-0294
Free subscription. Covers the automotive industry. Deals with all phases of the industry.

Chemicals

Chemical Processing
301 East Erie St., Chicago, IL 60611
Phone: 312-644-2020, fax: 312-644-1131
Free subscription. Covers the chemical industry. Frequent articles on risks assessments and environmental and safety issues. Deals with international regulations.

Hydrocarbon Processing
Gulf Publishing Company, 3301 Allen Parkway, Houston, TX 77019-1805
Phone: 713-529-4301, fax: 713-520-4433
Subscription $36 per year. Covers the hydrocarbon production industry. Primary focus is on oil production, refinery, and petrochemical industry. Frequent articles on international harmonization. Monthly articles on training and management.

Today's Chemist at Work
ACS, 1155 16th St., Washington, D.C. 20036
Phone: 202-872-4572, fax: 202-872-4403
Free subscription. Covers the chemical industry. Frequent articles on environmental regulations and quality assurance. The update section reviews federal regulations.

Electrical and Electronic

Ceramic Industry
5900 Harper Road, Suite 109, Solon, OH 44139-9605
Phone: 216-496-9271, fax: 216-496-9121
Free subscription. Covers the ceramic industry. Articles on quality, testing, and processing.

Cleanrooms
Penwell Publishing, Ten Tara Blvd., 5th Floor, Nashua, NH 03062-2801
Phone: 603-891-0123, fax: 603-891-9200
Free subscription. Covers clean rooms. Frequent articles on the new harmonized standards for clean rooms. Covers the medical and food industries as well as the electronics industry.

EE (Evaluation Engineering)
2504 N. Tamiami Trail, Nokomis, FL 34275-3482
Phone: 941-966-9521, fax: 941-966-2500
Free subscription. Covers electrical testing and evaluation. Frequently has articles on the new harmonized standards and quality assurance.

Electronic Packaging & Production
Cahners Publishing, 8773 South Ridgeling Blvd., Highlands Ranch, CO 80126-2329
Free subscription. Covers electronic packaging and interconnects. Will have articles on cleaning processes and standards.

EMC: Testing and Design
P.O. Box 41528, Nashville, TN 37204-9957

Phone: 303-220-0600

Free subscription. Covers EMC application, design, and testing. Excellent articles on EMC and harmonized standards.

InTech
ISA: International Society for Measurements and Control, P.O. Box 12277, Research Triangle Park, NC 27709

Phone: 919-549-8411, fax: 919-549-8288

Free subscription. Good source for information on international standards and documentation of procedures.

Printed Circuit Fabrications
P.O. Box 4200-40, Palm Coast, FL 32142-0040

Phone: 770-952-1303, fax: 770-952-6461

Free subscription. Covers the printed circuit board industry. Frequent articles on testing and international standards.

SMT
IHS Publishing Group, P.O. Box 159, Libertyle, IL 60048-5924

Phone: 847-362-8711, fax: 847-362-3484

Free subscription. Covers the electronic packaging industry. Articles on standards, procedures, and quality.

Testing and Measurement
P.O. Box 7601, Highland Ranch, CO 80126-9401

Free subscription. Covers electronic testing and quality assurance.

Environmental

American Environmental Laboratory
International Scientific Communications, Inc., P.O. Box 870, Shelton, CT 06484-0870

Phone: 203-926-9300, fax: 203-926-9310

Free subscription. Covers test methods. Good coverage on the establishment of a national accreditation system by the U.S. government.

Pollution Engineering
1350 E. Touhy Ave., Des Plaines, IL 60018-3358

Phone: 847-390-2615, fax: 847-390-2636

Free subscription. Covers pollution control. Articles on ISO 14000 and EPA regulations. Also handles books and standards.

International

European
200 Gray's Inn Road, London, WC1X 8NE
Phone: 1-800-875-2997, fax: 1-201-627-5872
Subscription $135 per year. Weekly newspaper on the EU. Covers the political situations.

International Business
IB Communications, 9 East 40th St., New York, NY 10016
Phone: 212-683-2426, fax: 212-683-3426
Free subscription. Covers international business. Articles on EU and trade regulations. Does a good job of covering the basics of international trade.

World Trade
Freedom Magazines, 17702 Cowan, Irvine, CA 92714
Phone: 714-798-3500, fax: 714-798-3501
Free subscription. Covers international business. Deals with cultural and business practices for successful international trade relations.

Machinery

Machine Design
1100 Superior Ave., Cleveland, OH 44134
Phone: 216-696-7000, fax: 216-696-8469
Free subscription. Covers the machine design industry. Deals with international requirements.

MAN
Nelson Publishing Co., 2504 N. Tamiami Trail, Nokomis, FL 34275-3482
Phone: 941-966-9521, fax: 941-966-2590
Covers the tool and manufacturing industry. Most of the articles take an advertisement approach, but they often discuss quality and operational procedures.

Plastic Technology
Bill Communications, 355 S. Park Ave., New York, NY 10010
Phone: 212-592-6570, fax: 212-592-6579

Free subscription. Covers all plastic technology. Articles on process control, equipment, and software. Covers international materials and equipment.

Plastic World
PTN Publishing Co., 445 Broad Hollow Road, Melville, NY 11747
Phone: 516-845-2700, fax: 516-845-7109
Free subscription. Covers the plastic design, material, and fabrication industry. Frequent articles and process checklists. Also reviews computer tracking systems and the CAMPUS harmonized material standards program.

Medical

IVD Technology
Cannon Communication, Inc., 3340 Ocean Park Blvd., Suite 1000, Santa Monica, CA 90405
Phone: 310-392-5509, fax: 310-392-4920
Free subscription. Covers the in-vitro diagnostic industry. Frequent articles on compliance issues, primarily on the FDA.

Medical Device and Diagnostic Industry
Cannon Communication, Inc., 3340 Ocean Park Blvd., Suite 1000, Santa Monica, CA 90405
Phone: 310-392-5509, fax: 310-392-4920
Free subscription. Covers the medical device industry. Frequent articles on compliance issues, primarily on the FDA.

Medical Plastics and Biomaterial
Cannon Communications, Inc., 3340 Ocean Park Blvd., Suite 1000, Santa Monica, CA 90405
Phone: 310-392-5509, fax: 310-392-4920
Free subscription. Covers medical and biocompatibility. Information is especially useful in process documentation.

Pharmaceutical

American Laboratory
P.O. Box 3095, Lowell, MA 01853-9816
Phone: 203-926-9300, fax: 203-926-9310
Free subscription. Covers equipment and testing procedures. Has been running editorials on establishing a national laboratory accreditation system.

Applied Clinical Trails
Advanstar, 859 Williamette St., Eugene, OR 97401-6806
Phone: 541-343-1200, fax: 541-344-3514
Free subscription. Covers conducting clinical trails. Reports monthly on the ICH standards and EU status.

Pharmaceutical Engineering
International Society for Pharmaceutical Engineering, 3816 W. Linebaug Ave., Suite 412, Tampa, FL 38624
Phone: 813-960-2105, fax: 813-960-2816
Free subscription. Covers pharmaceutical engineering. Articles on GMP and SOP for manufacturing of drugs.

Pharmaceutical Technology
Advanstar, P.O. Box 10460, Eugene, OR 87440-3622
Phone: 800-346-0085
Free subscription. Covers the pharmaceutical industry. Articles on GMP, ISO 9000, and quality assurance.

Quality

Compliance Engineering
One Tech Drive, Andover, MA 01810-9983
Phone: 508-681-6600, fax: 508-681-6637
Free subscription. Covers regulatory compliance with emphasis on the electrical and medical industries. The focus is on EU compliance.

Inform
Association for Information and Image Management International, 1100 Wayne Ave., Silver Spring, MD 20910
Phone: 301-587-8202
Subscription $80 per year. Covers documentation and protocols for storing and retrieving information. Good source for guidelines and help with documentation.

ISO Bulletin
Promotion and Press Dept., Case postule 56, CH-1211, Geneva 20 Switzerland
There is a charge for the subscription. Published by ISO. Provides reviews and status reports on standards.

Quality
Chilton Publications, 191 S. Gary Ave., Carol Stream, IL 60188
Phone: 708-665-1000, fax: 708-665-2225
Free subscription. Covers quality issues.

Quality Update
Irwin Publishing Company, 50 Main St., Suite 403, Fairfax, VA 22030
Phone: 703-591-9008, fax: 703-591-0971
$595 per year. Monthly coverage of ISO 9000. Good source for information.
Publishes a monthly list of companies that have become ISO 9000 registered.

Telecommunications

Lightwave
PennWell, Ten Tara Blvd., Nashua, NH 03062-2801
Phone: 603-891-0123, fax: 918-832-9295
Free subscription. Covers fiber optics communication. Monthly regulatory and
standards column. Frequent articles on standards and testing methods.

Satellite
Intertec Publishing Corp., P.O. Box 41369, Nashville, TN 37204-9913
Phone: 202-544-5895, fax: 202-544-0358
Free subscription. Covers satellite communications. Publishes a series of ar-
ticles on assignment of frequency and deregulation in the United States and the
EU.

St. Lucie Press
2000 Corporate Blvd., N.W., Boca Raton, FL 33431-9868
Phone: 561-994-0555, fax: 800-374-3401
E-mail address: information@slpress.com
Web site address: http://www.slpress.com
Provides all the EU Directives in an easy-to-use format, as well as many other
books on compliance.

Telecommunications International
BPA, 685 Canton St., Norwood, MA 02062
Phone: 617-356-4595, fax: 617-762-9071
Free subscription. Covers the EU telecommunications industry.

Professional Societies

American Society for Non-Destructive Testing
1711 Arlingate Lane, P.O. Box 28516, Columbus, OH 43229-0518
Phone: 614-274-6003, fax: 614-274-6899

American Society for Quality Control (ASQC)
P.O. Box 3005, Milwaukee, WI 43228-0519
Phone: 800-248-1946, fax: 414-272-1734

American Society for Testing of Materials (ASTM)
100 Bar Harbor Drive, Conshocken, PA 19428
Phone: 610-832-9500, fax: 610-832-9555

Association for the Advancement of Medical Instruments (AAMI)
3330 Washington Blvd., Suite 400, Arlington, VA 22201
Phone: 800-332-2264, fax: 703-276-4598

International Society for Measurements and Control (ISA)
P.O. Box 12277, Research Triangle Park, NC 27709
Phone: 919-549-8411, fax: 919-549-8288

International Society for Pharmaceutical Engineering (ISPE)
3816 W. Linebaug Ave., Suite 412, Tampa, FL 38624
Phone: 813-960-2105, fax: 813-960-2816

Standards

ANSI
11 W. 42nd St., New York, NY 10036
Phone: 212-642-4900, fax: 212-302-1286
Source for official international standards.

Commission of the European Communities
2100 M St. NW, Suite 707, Washington, D.C. 20037
Phone: 202-862-9599, fax: 202-429-1766
Provides a full range of information and pamphlets on the EU.

Global Engineering Documents
2805 McGaw Ave., Irvine, CA 92714
Phone: 800-854-7179, fax: 714-261-7892
Source for U.S. and international standards.

International Quality Press
321 N. Union St., Middletown, PA 17057
Phone: 717-930-0201
Source for all U.S. and international standards.

UNIPUB
4611-F Assembly Drive, Lanham, MA 20706
Phone: 800-233-0504, fax: 301-459-0056
Official source for EU publications.

Federal Agencies

Department of Commerce National Institutes of Standards and Technology (NIST)
Building 101, Room A903, Gaithersburg, MD 20889
Phone: 301-975-2762, fax: 301-975-1630

Food and Drug Administration (FDA)
Phone: 202-219-7316, fax: 202 260-7906
Many addresses listed. Call for information on which address can provide the specific information you need.

EU Institutions

European Commission
Headquarters: Rue de la Loi 200, 1049 Brussels
Phone: (32.2) 299.11.11
Web site: http://www.europa.eu.int

European Council
175 Rue de la Loi, 1048 Brussels
Phone: (32.2) 285.61.11, fax: 285.73.97/73.81

European Court of Auditors
Headquarters: 12, Rue Alcide De Gasperi, L-1615 Luxembourg
Phone: (352) 4398-518, fax: (352) 4398-430
Members: 15, one per Member State

The Court of Justice of the European Communities
L-2925 Luxembourg
Phone: (352) 4303-1, fax: (352) 4303-2600
Court of Justice: 15 judges and 9 advocates general
Court of First Instance: 15 judges

Web Site for EU Agencies and Bodies

Welcome to the home page of the Agencies, Foundations and Centers set up by a European Commission or a European Council decision but working entirely as autonomous bodies.

For further information please contact them individually. Links to new servers will be introduced periodically.

European Agency for the Evaluation of Medicinal Products (E.M.E.A.)
Website http://www.eurda.org

In a real single market, pharmaceutical products should be marketed with identical conditions of usage, and should benefit from an independent and experienced and scientifically based evaluation, protecting both the consumer and the industry. With its base in London, E.M.E.A. became operational on 1 January 1995.

European Agency for the Evaluation of Medicinal Products server describes its detailed objectives and tasks. It provides information on the new procedures for authorizing medicinal products in the EU as well as the telephone numbers and addresses of essential contact people. You will also find information on the Committee for Proprietary Medicinal Products (CPMP), as well as the Committee for Veterinary Medicinal Products (CVMP) which was set up to assist E.M.E.A.

7 Westferry Circus, Canary Wharf, UK-E14 4 HB London, United Kingdom
Tel: (44-171) 418 84 00   Fax: (44-171) 418 84 16
E-mail: mail@emea.eudra.org

European Environment Agency (EEA)
Website http://www.eea.dk

The EEA and its wider network, EIONET, were set up in Copenhagen in 1994 in order to deliver high quality environmental information to the Member States of the European Union, as well as to the general public. The main aims of the

Agency are to describe the present and foreseeable state of the environment as well as to provide relevant information for the implementation of Community's environment policy.

The European Environment Agency server provides information on EEA's missions and expectations; products and services; and organization and staff. You will find a presentation page of the EEA's wider data management team, EIONET, as well as links to other relevant environmental Web servers. An executive summary of the fifth Action Program on the environment in the European Union and a summary of the main European issues concerning health and environment are both new additions to this server.

Kongens Nytorv, 6 - DK-1050 København, Denmark
Tel: (45) 33 36 71 00   Fax: (45) 33 36 71 99
General Information E-mail: info@eea.dk
Technical information E-mail: webmaster@eea.dk

European Training Foundation
Website: http://www.etf.it

The European Training Foundation was inaugurated in Turin, Italy in January 1995. This agency was set up to coordinate and support all EU activities in the field of post-compulsory education. This was part of the overall Phare and Tacis Programmes for economic restructuring in the Partner States of Central and Eastern Europe and Central Asia.

The European Training Foundation server provides information on its background, tasks and aims. A survey of the Partner States and a detailed description of the Tacis and Phare programs.

Villa Gualino, Viale Settimio Severo 63-67, I-10133 Torino, Italy
Tel: (39-11) 630 22 22   Fax: (39-11) 630 22 00
E-mail: info@etf.it

European Centre for the Development of Vocational Training (CEDEFOP)
Website http://www.cedefop.gr

CEDEFOP was established in Berlin in 1975, but has recently moved to Thessaloniki, Greece. The Centre is contributing to the development of vocational training in Europe through its academic and technical activities.

The European Centre for the Development of Vocational Training server provides information about the Centre, useful contact addresses and links to other relevant servers.

P.O. Box 27, GR-55102 Thessaloniki (Finikas), Greece
Tel: (30-31) 490 111   Fax: (30-31) 490 102
E-mail: webmaster@cedefop.gr

European Centre for Drugs and Drug Addiction (EMCDDA)

EMCDDA was established in 1994 and located in Lisbon. The Centre's aim is to provide objective, reliable and comparable information at European level concerning drugs, drug addiction and their consequences. As the drug phenomenon comprises many complex and closely interwoven aspects, the Centre has the task of providing an overall statistical, documentary and technical picture of the drug problem to the Member States and the Community Institutions as they embark on combat measures.

Palacete Mascarenhas, Rua Cruz de Santa Apolia No 23/25, P-1100 Lisboa, Portugal
Tel: (351-1) 813 13 18   Fax: (351-1) 813 17 11
E-mail: emcdda@individual.puug.pt

European Foundation for the Improvement of Living and Working Conditions

The European Foundation for the Improvement of Living and Working Conditions is an autonomous body established by the European Community by a Council of Ministers' decision in 1975. Located in Dublin, Ireland, its aim is to contribute to the planning and establishment of better working and living conditions through action designed to increase and disseminate knowledge likely to assist this development. Its principal task is to advise the Community institutions on foreseeable objectives and guidelines by forwarding in particular scientific information and technical data.

Loughlinstown House, Shankill, Co. Dublin, Ireland
Tel: (353-1) 282 68 88   Fax: (353-1) 282 64 56
E-mail: postmaster@eurofound.ie

Office for Harmonization in the Internal Market

OHIM (Trade Marks and Designs) began its work on 1 September 1994 in Alicante, Spain. The Office is responsible for the registration and subsequent administration of Community trade marks, and in the future Community designs, which have effect throughout the European Union. The aim of the OHIM is to contribute to harmonization in the internal market in the domain of intellectual property, and in particular, the domain of trade marks and designs.

20 Avenida dela Aguilera, E-03006 Alicante, Spain
Tel: (34-6) 513 91 46   Fax: (34-6) 513 91 59
X.400: P OAMI A 400NET C ES

Community Plant Variety Rights Office
The Community Plant Variety Rights Office is now operational since 27 April
1995, and is temporarily located in Brussels. It's an entirely independent body
of the European Union. The Office is exclusively responsible for the implementation of the new regime of Community plant variety rights, like patents and
copyrights. Since 27 April 1995, plant breeders may ask for protection throughout the European Union by a single application to the Community Plant Variety
Rights Office.

Temporary address: Rue de la Loi 102, B-1040 Bruxelles, Belgique
Tel: (322) 299 19 44   Fax: (322) 299 19 46

European Agency for Safety and Health at Work
The European Agency for Safety and Health at Work was launched on 27
October 1995 in Bilbao, Spain where it will be located. In order to encourage
improvements, especially in the working environment, as regards the protection
of the safety and health of workers as provided for in the Treaty, the aim of the
Agency is to provide the Community bodies, the Member States and those
involved with all relevant technical, scientific and economic information. The
Agency's first priority is to create a network linking up national information
networks and facilitate the provision of information in the field of safety and
health at work.

Temporary address: Commission Européenne DG V
Bâtiment Jean Monnet, rue Alcide de Gasperi, L-2920 Luxembourg,
G-D Luxembourg
Tel: (352) 4301-32734   Fax: (352) 4301-34511
E-mail: emma.heighton@lux.dg5.cec.be

Translation Centre for Bodies in the European Union
The Translation Centre for Bodies in the European Union was set up in 1994
in Luxembourg. The Centre is carrying out the necessary translations for the
bodies and agencies mentioned above, with the exception of the European
Centre for the Development of Vocational Training and the European Foundation for the Improvement of Living and Working Conditions.

rue Joseph Junck, L-1839 Luxembourg, G-D Luxembourg
Tel: (352) 49 55 85-1   Fax: (352) 49 55 85-220

Web Sites*

AIIM (Association for Information and Image Management International)
http://www.aiim.org
Information on document and imaging management, including software.

ANIS (American National Institute for Standards)
http://www.anis.org
Information on standards.

ASQC (American Society for Quality Control)
http://www.asqc.org
Information and lists of sources on quality control and ISO 9000.

AVICENNA (Medical Information Super Site)
http://www.avicenna.com
Variety of useful databases. Registration required, but it is free.

CenterWatch
http://www.centerwatch.com
Lists active clinical trails by category and disease, profiles of research centers, and links to dozens of other sites.

EMEA (European Agency for Medicine Evaluation)
http://www.eudra.org
Official site for the EU EMEA; packed with information and documents.

Europa
http://www.europa.eu.int
EU Commission official site. Provides all kinds of information on Commission activities. Contains links to many other sites.

FDA
http://www.fda.gov
Official site for the FDA. Provides information on FDA activities and hot-links to other Web sites.

FedWorld
http://www.fedworld.gov
Official site for the U.S. government. List thousands of documents and information on over 100 government sites.

---

* *Applied Clinical Trials,* August 1988, p. 41 (additional Web sites added).

Institute for Interconnecting and Packaging Electronics (IPC)
http://www.ipc.org
A comprehensive site on electronics and interconnects. Design, fabrication, and testing information.

MEDMARKET
http://www.medmarket.com
Contains information and links to both governmental and private companies in the medical device market.

NIH (National Institutes of Health)
http://www.nih.gov
NIH home page. Provides information on their programs and contacts.

PharminfoNet
http://www.pharminfo.com
A super site on disease, drugs, and press releases.

Quality Online
http://www.qualitymag.com
Information and trial software on quality and ISO 9000. Contains links to many other quality-related sites.

RAPS (Regulatory Affairs Professional Society)
http://www.medmarket.com/tenants/raps
Information on the society and sources of information on regulatory affairs.

St. Lucie Press
http://www.slpress.com
Provides lists of publications on the EU, ISO 9000, and quality areas.

Technomark
http://194.72.162.180/technomark/index.html
Information on Contract Research Organizations (CROs). Information on the company, publications, and CROs in other countries.

Appendix 4: EU Legal Requirements for Industrial Equipment and Consumer Goods*

By Brian P. Kujawa

Directive	Citation Number	Official Journal	Date of OJ	Current Status	Date of Implementation
General					
Extension of information procedures on standards and technical rules	83/189/EEC	L 100	4/26/83	Adopted	
(1st Amendment of Directive 83/189/EEC)	88/182/EEC	L 81	3/26/88	Adopted	1/1/89
(2nd Amendment of Directive 83/189/EEC)	94/10/EC	L 100	4/19/94	Adopted	
(Amendment—Updating List of National Standards Bodies)	Decision 96/139/EC	L 32	2/10/96	Adopted	Immed.
Modules of Conformity Assessment	Decision 93/465/EEC	L 220	8/30/93	Adopted	Immed.
Regulation No. 3052/95 Exchange of Information on National Measure	Decision 95/321/EC	L 321	12/30/95	Adopted	Immed.

*Current through February 15, 1996.

Directive	Citation Number	Official Journal	Date of OJ	Current Status	Date of Implementation
Good Laboratory Practices	88/320/EEC	L 320	6/9/88	Adopted	Immed.
(1st Amendment of 88/320/EEC)	87/18/EEC	L18	12/18/86		
(2nd Amendment of 88/320/EEC)	90/18/EC	L 18	12/18/89		
Uniform Surveillance Documentation	96/21/EC	L 21	1/27/96	Adopted	Immed.
Appliances Appliances burning gaseous fuels	90/396/EEC	L 196	7/7/90	Adopted	1/1/89
(Amendment—CE Marking)	93/68/EEC	L 220	8/30/93	Adopted	1/1/95
Notified Bodies	95/C 280/01	C 280	10/25/95	Communication	
Standards	94/C 334/08 95/C 187	C 334 C 187	11/30/94 7/27/95	Communications	
Civil Aviation Council Regulation on technical requirements in civil aviation	No. (EEC) 3922/91	L 373	12/31/91	Adopted	1/1/92
Construction Products	89/106/EEC	L 40	2/11/89	Adopted	6/28/91
(Amendment—CE Marking)	93/68/EEC	L 220	8/30/93	Adopted	1/1/95
Notified Bodies	95/C 280/01	C 280	10/25/95	Communication	
Interpretative documents for the implementation of Directive 89/106/EEC	94/C 62/01	C 62	2/28/94	Communication	
Decision implementing Article 20 of Directive 89/106/EEC	Decision 94/611/EC	L 241	9/16/94	Adopted	
Decision implementing Article 20 (2) of Directive 89/106/EEC	Decision 95/204/EC	L 129	6/2/95	Adopted	
(Corrigendum)	—	L 217	9/11/95		
Common Procedural Rules for European Technical Approval	Decision 94/23/EC	L 107	1/20/94	Adopted	

Directive	Citation Number	Official Journal	Date of OJ	Current Status	Date of Implementation
Notified Bodies	94/C 206/04	C 206	7/26/94	Communication	
	95/C 211	C 211	8/15/95		
Electrical Equipment					
Electrical equipment for use in potentially explosive atmospheres (supersedes Directives 76/117/EEC, 79/196/EEC, and 82/130/EEC)	94/9/EC	L 100	4/19/94	Adopted	7/1/2003
Notified Bodies Directive 76/117/EEC	94/C 80/06	C 80	3/17/94	Communications	
	95/C 215/02	C 215	8/19/95		
Standards (stated as annexes to Directives 79/196/EEC and 82/130/EEC as amended to adapt for technical progress)	Commission Directives 94/26/EC 94/44/EC	L 157 L 248	6/24/94 9/23/94	Adopted	7/14/94 10/13/94
Low Voltage Equipment					
Electrical appliances standards	73/23/EEC	L 77	3/26/73	Adopted	8/75
(Amendment—CE Marking)	93/68/EEC	L 220	8/30/93	Adopted	1/1/95
Notified Bodies and Symbols					
Revised Lists Amendment	92/C 210/01	C 210	8/15/92	Communications	
	95/C 214/02	C 214	8/18/95		
EN Standards and HDs	92/C 210/01	C 210	8/15/92		
	93/C 18/04	C 18	1/23/93		
	93/C 319/02	C 319	11/26/93	Communications	
	94/C 169/04	C 169	6/22/94		
	94/C 199/03	C 199	7/21/94		
Electromagnetic Compatibility					
Radio interference (L 127)	89/336/EEC	L 139	5/23/89	Adopted	7/1/88
(Amendment—Transition Period)	92/31/EEC	L 126	5/12/92	Adopted	10/28/92
(Amendment—CE Marking)	93/68/EEC	L 220	8/30/93	Adopted	1/1/95
Notified Bodies	95/C 280/01	C 280	10/25/95	Communication	

Directive	Citation Number	Official Journal	Date of OJ	Current Status	Date of Implementation
Standards	92/C 44/10	C 44	2/19/92	Communications	
	92/C 92/02	C 92	4/10/92	Communications	
	94/C 49/03	C 49	2/17/94		
	95/C 241/	C 241	9/16/95		
	95/C 325/05	C 325	12/6/95		
Instruments					
Non-automatic weighing machines	90/384/EEC	L 189	7/20/90	Adopted	7/1/92
(Amendment—CE Marking)	93/68/EEC	L 220	8/30/93	Adopted	1/1/95
Notified Bodies	95/C 280/01	C 280	10/25/95	Communication	
Standards	93/C 104/04	C 104	5/7/93	Communications	
	94/C 153/09	C 153	6/4/94		
Measuring Instruments and Means of Metrologic Control	71/316/EEC	L 202 [Eng. Spec. Ed.—1971 (II)]	9/6/71 (Dec. 1972)	Adopted	3/26/73
(Amendments—Ascension of UK and Ireland)	72/427/EEC	L 332 [Eng. Spec. Ed.—1972 (28–30 Dec.)]	12/28/72	Adopted	1/1/73
(Amendment—Technical Update)	83/575/EEC	L 332	11/28/83	Adopted	1/1/85
(Amendment—Update of Ireland Symbol)	87/354/EEC	L 192	7/11/87	Adopted	12/31/87
(Amendment—Ascension of Greece, Spain and Portugal)	87/355/EEC	L 192	7/11/87	Adopted	12/31/87
(Amendment—Technical Updates)	88/665/EEC	L 382	12/31/88	Adopted	12/31/88
(Amendment—EFTA Nations' Symbols)	94/C 320/06	C 320	11/17/94	Adopted	Immed.
Units of Measure	80/181/EEC	L 39	2/15/80	Adopted	10/1/81
(Amendment—Update)	85/1/EEC	L 2	1/3/85	Adopted	1/1/85?
(Amendment—Update)	89/617/EEC	L 357	12/7/89	Adopted	12/31/89

Directive	Citation Number	Official Journal	Date of OJ	Current Status	Date of Imple-mentation
(Proposed Update)	91/C 185/06	C 185	7/11/91	Proposal (Withdrawn?)	
Lifts Standards applied to electrically operated lifts	90/486/EEC	L 270	10/2/90	Adopted	
Safety requirements for lifting appliances for persons	95/16/EC	L 213	9/6/95	Adopted	
Medical Devices Electromedical equipment	84/539/EEC	L 300	11/19/84	Adopted	
(Amendment—Medical Devices)	93/42/EEC	L 169	6/18/93	Adopted	1/1/96
Active Implantable Medical Devices	90/385/EEC	L 189	7/20/90	Adopted	7/1/92
(Amendment—CE Marking)	93/68/EEC	L 220	8/30/93	Adopted	1/1/95
Notified Bodies	95/C 280/01	C 280	10/25/95	Communication	
Standards	94/C 277 95/C 204 95/C 307/09	C 277 C 204 C 307	10/4/94 8/9/95 11/18/95	Communications	
Medical Devices	93/42/EEC	L 169	6/18/93	Adopted	1/1/96
Notified Bodies	95/C 280/01	C 280	10/25/95	Communication	
Standards	94/C 277 95/C 204/ 95/C 307/09 95/C 307/10	C 277 C 204 C 307 C 307	10/4/94 8/9/95 11/18/95 11/18/95	Communications	
In-Vitro Diagnostic Devices	95/C 172/02	C 192	7/7/95	Proposal	
(Economic & Social Committee Opinion)	96/C 18/02	C 192	1/22/96		
Machinery	89/392/EEC	L 183	6/29/89	Adopted	12/31/92
(Amendment—Moving Machines [FOPs, ROPs])	91/368/EEC	L 198	7/22/91	Adopted	1/31/96
(Amendment—Lifting and Loading)	93/44/EEC	L 175	7/19/93	Adopted	1/1/97

Directive	Citation Number	Official Journal	Date of OJ	Current Status	Date of Implementation
(Amendment—CE Marking)	93/68/EEC	L 220	8/30/93	Adopted	1/1/95
Notified Bodies	95/C 280/01	C 280	10/25/95	Communication	
Standards	92/C 154/03	C 154	6/24/92	Communications	
	93/C 229/03	C 229	8/25/93		
	94/C 207/03	C 207	7/27/94		
	94/C 377/08	C 377	12/31/94		
	95/C 165/03	C 165	6/30/95		
	96/C 42/05	C 42	2/14/96		
Telecommunications Terminal Equipment Approximation of Member States' laws concerning telecommunications terminal equipment, including mutual recognition of their conformity	91/263/EEC	L 128	5/23/91	Adopted	11/6/92
(Amendment—CE Marking)	93/68/EEC	L 220	8/30/93	Adopted	1/1/95
Notified Bodies	95/C 280/01	C 280	10/25/95	Communication	
Standards (NETs) (under predecessor, Directive 86/361/EEC)	89/C 210/02	C 210	8/16/89	Communications	
	92/C 143/03	C 143	6/5/92		
	93/C 53/05	C 53	2/24/93		
(Supplement—satellite earth stations)	93/97/EEC	L 290	11/24/93	Adopted	
Supplement ONP	96/C266/95	C 266	10/13/95	Adopted	
(Implementation—general attachment requirements for public pan-European cellular digital land-based mobile communications)	Decision 94/11/EC	L 8	1/12/94	Adopted	
(Implementation— telephony application requirements for public pan-European cellular digital land-based mobile communications)	Decision 94/12/EC	L 8	1/12/94	Adopted	

Directive	Citation Number	Official Journal	Date of OJ	Current Status	Date of Implementation
(Implementation—attachment requirements for terminal equipment interface for ONP 2,048 kbits/s digital unstructured leased lines)	Decision 94/470/EC	L 194	7/29/94	Adopted	
(Implementation—general terminal attachment requirements for Digital European Cordless Tele-communications [DECT])	Decision 94/471/EC	L 194	7/29/94	Adopted	
(Implementation—telephony application requirements for Digital European Cordless Tele-communications [DECT])	Decision 94/472/EC	L 194	7/29/94	Adopted	
(Implementation—requirements for terminal equipment interface for ONP 64 kbits/s digital un-structured leased lines)	Decision 94/821/EC	L 339	12/29/94	Adopted	
(Implementation—general terminal attachment requirements for Digital European Cordless Tele-communications [DECT], public access profile [PAP] applications)	Decision 95/525/EC	L 300	12/13/95	Adopted	
Telecommunication Mobile & personnel communications	Resolution (95/C 188/02)	C 188	6/29/95		
Proposal on (ONP)	Proposal 95/C 112/04	C 122	5/18/95		
(ONP) Networks	Common Position 95/C 28/01	C 281	10/25/95		

Directive	Citation Number	Official Journal	Date of OJ	Current Status	Date of Implementation
(Implementation—attachment requirements for hand-set terminals for ISDN; telephony 3.1 kHz teleservices)	Decision 95/526/EC	L 300	12/13/95	Adopted	
Personal Protection Equipment	89/686/EEC	L 399	12/30/89	Adopted	12/1/91
(Amendment—CE Marking)	93/68/EEC	L 220	8/30/93	Adopted	1/1/95
(Amendment—two-wheeled motor vehicle helmets and transition period)	93/95/EEC	L 276	11/9/93	Adopted	6/30/95
(Proposed Amendment—Repeal of year CE Marking affixed requirement)	96/C 23/07	C 23	1/27/96	Proposal	
Notified Bodies	95/C 280/01	C 280	10/25/95	Communication	
Standards	92/C 44/10	C 44	2/19/92	Communications	
	92/C 240/05	C 240	9/19/92		
	93/C 345/05	C 345	12/23/93		
	94/C 359/06	C 359	12/16/94		
	95/C 224/03	C 224	8/30/95		
	96/C 7/09	C 7	1/8/96		
Health and safety requirements for the use by workers of personal protective equipment at the workplace (3rd Directive within the meaning of Article 16 (1) of Directive 89/391/EEC)	89/656/EEC	L 393	12/30/89	Adopted	
(Implementation)	89/C 328/02	C 328	12/30/89	Communication	
Toys (approximation of the laws of Member States on the safety of toys)	88/378/EEC	L 187	7/16/88	Adopted	6/30/95
(Amendment—CE Marking)	93/68/EEC	L 220	8/30/93	Adopted	1/1/95

Directive	Citation Number	Official Journal	Date of OJ	Current Status	Date of Imple- mentation
Notified Bodies	95/C 280/01	C 280	10/25/95	Communication	
Standards	89/C 155/02	C 155	6/23/89	Communications	
	90/C 154/03	C 154	6/23/90		
	93/C 237/02	C 237	8/30/93		
	94/C 129/13	C 129	5/11/94		
	95/C 156/04	C 156	6/22/95		
	95/C 265/05	C 265	10/12/95		
Simple Pressure Vessels	87/404/EEC	L 220	8/8/87	Approved	7/1/90
(Amendment—Transition Period)	90/488/EEC	L 270	10/2/90	Approved	7/1/92
(Amendment—CE Marking)	93/68/EEC	L 220	8/30/93	Approved	1/1/95
Notified Bodies	95/C 280/01	C 280	10/25/95	Communication	
Standards	92/C 104/04	C 104	4/24/94	Communications	
	95/C 162/04	C 162	6/27/95		
Product Liability	85/374/EEC	L 210	8/7/85	Adopted	7/1/88
Access of consumers to justice and the settlement of consumer disputes in the Single Market	COM (93) 576 final	N/A	11/16/93	Commission Green Paper	
(Economic and Social Committee Opinion)	94/C 295/01	C 295	10/22/94		
General Product Safety	92/59/EEC	L 228	8/11/92	Adopted	7/1/95
Protection of individuals with regard to the processing of personal data and the free movement of such data	95/46/EC	L 281	11/23/95	Adopted	11/23/98
Worker Safety	89/391/EEC	L 183	6/29/89	Adopted	
Minimum safety and health for work equipment used by workers at work (1st Directive within the meaning of Article 16 (1) of Directive 89/391/EEC)	89/654/EEC	L 393	12/30/89	Adopted	12/31/92

Directive	Citation Number	Official Journal	Date of OJ	Current Status	Date of Imple-mentation
Minimum safety and health for work equipment used by workers in the workplace (2nd Directive within the meaning of Article 16 (1) of Directive 89/391/EEC)	89/655/EEC	L 393 L 59	12/30/89	Adopted Corrigendum	12/31/92
(Amendment)	92/57/EEC	L 245	8/26/92	Adopted	
(Amendment)	94/C 104 95/C 246	C 104 C 246	4/12/94 9/22/95	Proposal Amended Prop.	
Manual handling of loads where there is a risk particularly of back injury (4th Directive within the meaning of Article 16 (1) of Directive 89/391/EEC)	90/269/EEC	L 156	6/21/90	Adopted	12/31/92
Visual display units (including workstations) (5th Directive within the meaning of Article 16 (1) of 89/391/EEC)	90/270/EEC	L 156	6/21/90	Adopted	12/31/92
Risks related to exposure to carcinogens at work (6th Directive within the meaning of Article 16 (1) of Directive 89/391/EEC)	90/394/EEC	L 197	7/26/90	Adopted	
Risks related to exposure to biological agents at work (7th Directive within the meaning of Article 16 (1) of Directive 89/391/EEC)	90/679/EEC	L 374	12/31/90	Adopted	11/09/93
(Amendment—genetically modified biological agents)	93/88/EEC	L 268	10/29/93	Adopted	4/30/94
(Amendment)	95/	L 155	6/30/95	Adopted	
Temporary or mobile construction sites (8th Directive within the meaning of Article 16 (1) of Directive 89/391/EEC)	92/27/EEC	L 245	8/26/92	Adopted	

Directive	Citation Number	Official Journal	Date of OJ	Current Status	Date of Imple-mentation
Provision of safety and/or health signs at work (9th Directive within the meaning of Article 16 (1) of Directive 89/391/EEC)	92/58/EEC	L 245	8/26/92	Adopted	
Protection of workers in surface and underground mineral-extracting industries (12th Directive within the meaning of Article 16 (1) of Directive 89/391/EEC)	92/104/EEC	L 404	12/31/92	Adopted	
Risks arising from physical agents	93/C 77/02	C 77	3/18/93	Proposal	
Safety of Recreational Craft	94/25/EC	L 164	6/30/94	Adopted	
Standards	95/C 255/	C 255	9/30/95	Communication	
Energy Labeling (Directive on the indication by labeling and standard product information of the consumption of energy and other resources by house-hold appliances)	92/75/EEC	L 297	10/13/92	Adopted	
(Implementation—electric ovens)	79/531/EEC	L 531	6/13/79	Adopted	6/1981
(Implementation—house-hold electric refrigerators, freezers and their combinations)	Commission Directive 94/2/EC	L 45	2/17/94	Adopted	3/9/94
(Proposed Directive— energy efficiency require-ments for household electric refrigerators, freezers and their combinations)	94/C 390 96/C 49/07	C 390 C 49	12/31/94 2/20/96	Proposal Amended Prop.	
(Implementation—energy efficiency requirements for household electric washing machines)	Commission Directive 95/12/EC	L 136	6/8/95	Adopted	6/28/95

Directive	Citation Number	Official Journal	Date of OJ	Current Status	Date of Imple- mentation
Standards	95/C 312/05	C 312	11/23/95	Communication	
(Implementation—energy efficiency requirements for household clothes dryers)	Commission Directive 95/13/EC	L 136	6/8/95	Adopted	6/28/95
Standards	95/C 312/06	C 312	11/23/95	Communication	

Glossary

Accompanying Document—Any document required by a directive to physically accompany a product when it is placed on the market.

Accreditation—Procedure whereby an authoritative body gives formal recognition that an organization or person is qualified to carry out specific tasks.

Agency—An administrative body for a set of specific directives, such as EUROATOM, which administers radioactive products. The EU sets up agencies in specific areas that have a large number of directives. The Notified Bodies for the directives fall under the agencies.

AIMD—Abbreviation for *Active Implantable Medical Device Directive.*

Assessment Factor—An expression of the degree of uncertainty in extrapolation from test data on a limited number of species to the real environment. It indicates the probability that test data are correct.

Association Agreement—An agreement with a country outside the EU. Associate countries accept most of the EU Directives as law and they receive aid from the EU. There are over 70 associate countries.

Audit—The formal independent review of a process, activity, or system conducted to compare the performance of various activities to a recognized standard.

Authoritative Body—A national agency or body established to give formal recognition to an organization or person to carry out specific evaluations.

Authorized Representative—The legal person established within the Community who may substitute for the manufacturer in legal matters between the manufacturer and the authorities and bodies in the EU. It is usually the manufacturer's distributor in the EU.

Basic Patent—The patent that grants market protection and prevents others from duplicating the effort. In the market authorization, the manufacturer must designate which patent is the basic patent.

Batch—A defined amount of starting material or packaging material processed into a homogeneous product.

BATCH—The symbol for batch number in the EU.

Batch Number—A distinctive combination of numbers and/or letters which specifically identifies a batch and maintains its traceability.

Biological Test—A test in which the results are based on measurements on a living organism or process.

Calibration—The set of operations which establishes the relationship between values indicated by a measuring instrument or system and the corresponding known value of the reference standard.

Cassis de Dijon—The pivotal court case in the EU which forced the Member States to follow the provisions for the free movement of goods in the EU Treaty.

CB Scheme—A laboratory program accredited by the International Electrotechnical Commission to give a CB Test Certificate to a manufacturer for a product. The test results and certificate will be recognized by all member countries. The certificate is to be used for market authorization. If testing is done by a member of the CB Scheme, the tests do not have to be repeated in other member countries.

CB Test Certificate—A certified form given by a member of the CB Scheme to a manufacturer which guarantees that the product conforms to the technical standards that apply. With it, the product can be sold in any member country without retesting.

CCITT—Abbreviation for International Telegraph and Telephone Committee under the auspices of the International Telecommunications Union (ITU). It is a United Nations organization. Its aim is to foster international cooperation in telecommunication. CISPR is a subcommittee.

CE Marking of Conformity—A blanket mark stating that a product meets all the EU regulatory requirements.

CE Marking

CEN—Abbreviation for Committee for European Norms. It is also referred to as the European Commission for Standardization. It develops the non-electrical standards for determining product compliance.

CENELEC—Abbreviation for the European Commission for Electrotechnical Standardization. It develops the electrical standards for product compliance.

Certificate of Compliance—A notification that a competent product or service conforms to the EU Directives.

Certificate of Conformity—See *Certificate of Compliance.*

Certification—Procedures by which a third party gives written assurance that a product or service conforms to specified requirements.

Certification Body—Notified Body or registrar designated by the EU.

Class I Device—Medical device which does not enter into contact or interact with the body.

Class IIa Device—Medical device which is invasive in its interaction with the human body.

Class IIb Device—Medical device which is either partially or totally implantable within the human body.

Class III Device—Medical device which affects the functioning of vital organs.

Clean Area—An enclosed area with defined environmental control of particles and microbial contamination. It is constructed so as to reduce the introduction, generation, and retention of contaminants within the area.

Clinical Investigation—The process of verifying that the performance of a medicinal product conforms to its intended use. It is also the process of determining any side effects and whether the risks of those side effects outweigh the benefits of the intended use of the product.

Clinical Trial—A controlled dosage testing of a medicinal product on a human or animal.

Commission—Its primary function is to implement the directives. It can propose directives to the EU Council and additions to the budget to the Assembly.

Committee of the Regions—Made up of key local politicians. Their opinions are given a great deal of weight by the Parliament, Council, and Commission. All local infrastructure programs originate from and are supervised by this committee. Public utilities, regional development, land utilization, energy, education programs, and funding are reviewed by this committee.

Competent Authority—A national agency of an EU member country which determines non-compliance of products and processes. The committee also provides technical evaluations for the EU. Also called a National Authority.

Competent Body—A laboratory accredited by the International Electrotechnical Commission and authorized by an EU Competent Authority to give a CB Test Certificate to a manufacturer for a product.

Compliance—The official act of meeting specific requirements.

Component—A mechanical, optical, or electrical subsection, part, or piece of machinery, apparatus, or an appliance. In many directives, the definition changes to those pieces whose failure causes injury.

Conference of Committee Chairmen—Prepares the agendas for Parliamentary committees and coordinates works with the Council, the Commission, and the Standing Committees.

Conference of Presidents—Maintains relationships with governments of third countries. It is a subcommittee of the Commission.

Council—A legislative and executive body of the EU. Its primary function is to write directives and regulations. The membership changes depending upon the topic.

Court of Auditors—The institution that reviews the financial transactions of the EU and its agencies. It has the authority to audit anyone who provides services or products to the EU.

Court of First Instance—Handles cases brought by individuals and businesses. Appeals are handled by the Court of Justice.

Court of Justice—Decides all cases of infringement. Cases can be referred by the Commission or Member States' courts.

Customer—The recipient of a product or service.

Custom Union—The term used by the EU to designate all the export and import custom officials and organizations within each Member State responsible for enforcing the EU Directives and standards.

Danger Zone—Any zone within and/or around machinery in which the health or safety an exposed person is subject to risk.

Decision—A ruling made on an issue brought before the Commission.

Declaration of Conformity—The part of a written quality assurance procedure in which a manufacturer states that the product conforms to all the relevant EU Directives.

Declaration of Design Conformity—A certificate stating that the design of a product conforms to the EU Directives. It is issued by a Notified Body after reviewing the design information.

De Facto Technical Regulations—Competent Authority rulings, requirements, provisions, or protocols that must be followed to market a product. Generally, they are not included in the technical standard.

Design Verification—The process for ensuring that a product is designed to meet the requirements in the EU Directives.

Device for Performance Evaluation—Any device intended by the manufacturer to be subject to one or more performance evaluation studies in clinical laboratories or in other appropriate environments outside of the manufacturer's premises.

Directives—The laws of the EU.

Directorates-General—Subcommittees of the Commission. One of their primary functions is to publish draft directives for public comment and review. They also are responsible for disseminating information on reported non-compliances to the Member States and maintaining surveillance reports. This is done electronically, and results can be in the hands of the Member States within five working days. Their duties also involve providing staffing to the Council.

Draft Standard—A document which contains the proposal for a technical standard concerning a given subject being considered for adoption by a standards body and the Standing Committee. It is circulated for public comment. It is designated by "PR" (e.g., PREN 1005).

Dust Explosive Atmosphere—Symbol for equipment used in potentially explosive atmospheres in which the primary hazard is dust.

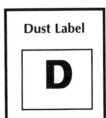

Dust Label

D

EAD—see *PEA*.

EC—European Community, now called the European Union.

ECO-Label—Symbol that a product is environmental friendly and energy efficient.

EC-Type—A product that has been tested and confirmed by a Notified Body to meet the EU Directives.

EC-Type Certificate—A set of specifications which state the requirements for a product to become an EC-Type.

EC Type-Examination—Testing performed by a Notified Body which proves that a device is in compliance with the relevant EU Directives.

EEA—Abbreviation for the European Economic Area. See also *European Economic Area.*

EEC—Abbreviation for the European Economic Community. It was the original name of the EU.

EFTA—Abbreviation for European Free Trade Area. Consisted of Austria, Finland, Liechtenstein, Norway, Sweden, and Switzerland. The European Free Trade Area merged with the EU on January 1, 1994. Switzerland did not join the EU, but became a member of the EEA instead.

EINECS—Abbreviation for European Inventory of Existing Commercial Substances. It is a list of chemicals sold within the EU.

Symbol for the EMEA

EMEA—Abbreviation for the European Medicine Evaluation Agency. It is the agency responsible for medicinal products. The Standing Committees now fall under this agency.

EMC—Abbreviation for the *Electro-Magnetic Compatibility Directive.*

Emission—Electromagnetic energy radiated by an electrical circuit or equipment.

EN—Abbreviation for European Norm, which is a test standard.

EOTA—Abbreviation for European Organization for Technical Approvals. This organization grants European Technical Approvals, fosters mutual recognition of test results within and outside of the EU, and drafts guidelines for directives and standards.

Essential Requirements—The safety factors that a product must meet to be sold in the EU. They are stated in the directives.

ETA—Abbreviation for European Technical Approval. It is issued by EOTA or a Notified Body to certify that a product meets the EU Directives. ETAs are used for products to which the harmonized standards do not apply.

ETSI—Abbreviation for Electro-Technical Standards Institute. ETSI writes electrical and telecommunication standards.

EU—European Union. Formerly the European Community (EC). Formed by the addition of Austria, Finland, and Sweden to the original Member States.

EU Commission—See *Commission.*

EU Council—The main council of the EU. It is comprised of the heads of state of the Member States. See also *Council.*

EUROATOM—Abbreviation for the European Atomic Energy Commission. It regulates nuclear products.

Flag of the EU
(white stars on a
blue background)

European Economic Area—Designation for countries that were members of the EFTA. The EEA was formed after the EFTA merged with the EU. Members of the EEA agree to combine economically, but not culturally or for purposes of defense. Its members are Switzerland, Liechtenstein, Norway, and Iceland.

European Pharmacopoeia—The official standards for medicinal products. Formed by the Treaty of Brussels. It was the first attempt toward economic unity in Europe.

European Political Cooperative—An agreement signed between members of the EC in which they agree to cooperate on matters of foreign policy. It is now mandatory for members of the EU.

EU Treaty—Treaty passed in November 1992. It established the modern European Union.

EU Verification—The process used by a Notified Body to confirm that a product meets EU requirements.

Explosive Atmosphere—Mixture of dust, gas, mist, particles, or vapor with air which might burn violently and extremely rapidly if ignited.

Exposed Person—Any person wholly or partially in the danger zone.

Exposure Assessment—An assessment of the effects and metabolic fates of a substance in order to estimate the dosage to which a human population or the environment is likely to be exposed. The assessment should take into account the human population or environmental components.

Finished Product—A product that has undergone all stages of production, including packaging, and is in its final shipping container.

Foreseeable Event—The probability of the occurrence of an event that must be prevented. It must be identified in the risks assessment. For example, the removal of a guard from a machine.

Foreseeable Lifetime—The manufacturer's designated lifetime projection under normal operations used to establish the design criteria for an apparatus, component, piece of equipment, or machinery. It must be included in the TCF.

Free Movement of Goods—One of the three pillars of the EU Treaty. One of the major tenets of the EU is no restrictions on the movement of goods from one Member State to another.

Gas Explosive Atmosphere—Symbol for protection against a potentially explosive gas atmosphere.

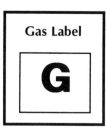

GATT—Abbreviation for General Agreement on Tariffs and Trade. Under GATT, there is a notification scheme for regulations and standards that will affect international trade.

GCP—Abbreviation for *Good Clinical Practices,* which are guidelines for clinical trials. By following these guidelines, retesting is not necessary in any member of the ICH.

GLP—Abbreviation for *Good Laboratory Practices,* which are guidelines for the testing of regulated products. ISO Guide 25 is the standard for the *GLP.*

GMP—Abbreviation for *Good Manufacturing Practices.*

Gross Contamination—Contamination of a starting material or a product with another material.

Harmonized Standard—A technical specification that has been adopted by either CEN or CENELEC. It states the procedure for supplying information regarding technical standards and regulations. Complying with harmonized standards gives a product the presumption of conformity to the essential requirements of the EU Directives.

High Voltage—Any voltage capable of igniting an explosive atmosphere.

ICH—Abbreviation for the International Conference on Harmonization. It develops harmonized standards in the medical field among its members. The three principal members are the United States, the EU, and Japan. Its most recent work is the new *GCP*.

IEC—Abbreviation for the International Electrotechnical Commission. It writes international electrical standards. ETSI is the EU's representative on the IEC.

IEC 68 Series—A series of standards for determining the environmental performance of equipment.

IEC 600 Series—A series of standards for medical devices and equipment.

IEC 1000 Series—A series of standards for determining the electromagnetic compatibility of electrical apparatus, equipment, or machinery.

Immunity—Protection from electromagnetic disturbance caused by the operation of a piece of electronic or electrical equipment.

In-Process Controls—Checks performed during production in order to ensure that a product conforms to its Certificate of Conformity.

Installation—The same as assembly. It is the point at which a product is "placed into service."

Intended Purpose—The expected use of a product, according to the manufacturer's label, instructions, and/or promotional material.

Intended Use—See *Intended Purpose.*

Intermediate Product—Partly processed material which must undergo further manufacturing steps before it becomes a bulk product.

Internal—From the company or supplier's point of view.

Internal Production Control—The quality plan that ensures a product satisfies the requirements of the directives that apply to it.

In-Vitro Test—A test to determine the physiological or health status of a human or animal.

ISO—Abbreviation for International Organization for Standardization. It is the body responsible for writing international generic standards. ISO is the final authority on standards in the EU.

ISO 9000 Standards—A set of international standards that provide generic guidelines against which a customer can evaluate the adequacy of a supplier's quality system.

ISO 14000—A set of international standards that provide generic guidelines for environmental management.

ITU—Abbreviation for International Telecommunications Union. It writes international standards for telecommunication.

IVD—Abbreviation for the *In-Vitro Diagnostic Device Directive*.

Lot—See *Batch.*

Lot Number—See *Batch Number.*

LVD—Abbreviation for the *Low Voltage Directive.*

Machinery—Any apparatus, equipment, or system which has at least one moving part that performs a function.

Management Review—The formal review and evaluation of the performance of a quality system and the recommendations for corrections to the quality system.

Mandate—The formal designation of a standards organization to develop standards for the EU.

Mandatory Certification—Certification required by a regulation, directive, or decision which must be performed in order to place a product on the market.

Manufacturer—The legally designated individual with responsibility for the design, production, packaging, and labeling of a device before it is placed on the market. This is the person in an organization who has final authority over the product. In the EU, it is the holder of a Manufacturing Authorization as described in Article 16 of Directive 75/319/EEC.

MDD—Abbreviation for the *Medical Device Directive.*

Measures—The rulings of a Standing Committee.

Medical Device—Any apparatus, including the software necessary for its proper utilization, that is intended by the manufacturer to be used on human beings in order to diagnose, treat, or prevent an injury or disease. It can also be a device which is used for the control of conception or to investigate, modify, or replace anatomy or physiologic processes. It is not a pharmaceutical agent, but can be used to help such an agent function.

Medicinal Product—Any substance or device that requires a drug to function which is intended for the diagnosis or treatment of a disease or injury in humans or animals. It applies only to pharmaceutical agents.

Medicine—See *Medicinal Product.*

Member States—The 15 countries that make up the EU.

Modules of Conformity Assessment—A series of options for a manufacturer to demonstrate compliance to a directive. Which module a manufacturer must use depends upon the degree of risk to health, safety, and the environment.

Module A: EC Declaration of Conformity—The manufacturer self-certifies compliance with a directive and submits a TCF to the Standing Committee.

Module B: EC Type-Examination—This module refers only to the design phase. The manufacturer submits a production module to a Notified Body for testing.

Module C: EC Declaration of Conformity to Type—Applies only to the production phase. A Notified Body must certify that the product is in compliance and issues an EC Type-Examination Certificate.

Module D: Production Quality Assurance—The Notified Body performs a third-party audit of the production system and performs an EC Type-Examination.

Module E: Product Quality Assurance—Requires the testing and examination of Module D plus registration to the ISO 9000 standards.

Module F: EC Verification—In conjunction with the EC Type-Examinations, the Notified Body checks and attests that the product is in conformity with the technical documents and that the production system is capable of producing the required quality product. Usually requires statistical verification.

Module G: EC Unit Verification—This module relates to both the design and production phases. It is normally applied to small-volume production units such as pressure vessels or process equipment. The Notified Body reviews the design and testing to ensure compliance. Requires ISO 9000 registration.

Module H: Full Quality Assurance—This module applies to both design and production. It requires registration to ISO 9001. The Notified Body approves the design, tests the product, and verifies system effectiveness to comply with the directives.

MOU—Abbreviation for Memorandum of Understanding. It is a written agreement among a number of organizations which covers specific activities of common interest. There are a number of MOUs among accredited testing bodies for mutual recognition of audits and test results.

NAMAS—Abbreviation for the National Accreditation Board for Laboratories. These laboratories are accredited both within the EU and internationally.

National Standard—A standard adopted by a national standardization body and made available to the public.

NB—Abbreviation for Notified Body.

NIST—Abbreviation for National Institute for Standards and Technology. It is the primary standards body for the United States.

Non-Regulated Products—Products or services not covered by an EU Directive. They are covered by mutually recognized national standards within the EU.

Notified Body—A government-sanctioned organization that can certify a quality system or product to determine that it meets EU requirements. It is a registrar or a certified laboratory.

OJ No. C—Abbreviation for the *Official Journal of the European Communities* (Information and Notice Series). All proposals for decisions and directives of the Council are published in it.

OJ No. L—Abbreviation for the *Official Journal of the European Communities* (Legislation Series). All decisions and directives of the Council are published in it.

Ombudsman—A Parliamentary official who handles questions from the public regarding legislation, operation of the institutes, and complaints.

Opinion—Non-binding interpretation or analysis of a directive or subject issued by the Council, Committee, or Commission. Opinions are used by the Courts to help decide rulings.

Other Requirements—A requirement other than technical imposed on a product for the purpose of protecting the customer and the environment.

Outline for Harmonization Directive—Directive written by the Council which established the "New Approach Directives" and harmonized standards.

Packaging—All operations, including filling and labeling, which a bulk product has to undergo to become a finished product.

Packaging Material—Any material used in enclosing a product.

PEA—Abbreviation for the *Equipment Used in Potentially Explosive Atmospheres Directive.*

Pharmaceutical—A chemical or natural product administered to treat an ailment in an animal or human. See also *Medicinal Product.*

Physico-Chemical—A test in which the results are based on measurement of a physical or chemical change.

Placing in Service—The first time a product or machinery is used for its intended purpose by the customer.

Placing on the Market—The first time a product is available in return for payment or free of charge with the intention of distributing on the Community market.

Potentially Explosive Atmosphere—An atmosphere that could develop an explosive condition.

PPE—Abbreviation for the *Personnel Protection Equipment Directive.*

PREN—A draft standard.

Pressure Equipment—Any equipment that is pressurized above 50 psi or subjected to rapid buildup in pressure. Must meet the *Pressure Equipment Directive* and be marked with the symbol N.

Prevention—All the steps or measures taken or planned at all stages of work in the undertaking to prevent or reduce occupational risks. This is the primary purpose of a risks assessment.

Procedures—Description of the operations involved in the preparation of a product or service.

Process—A set of interrelated activities, and their necessary resources, which transforms inputs into outputs.

Process Verification—The procedures for proving that a process is performing as expected and the output is in compliance with the appropriate standards and directives.

Product—The output of processes. It can be hardware, software, or a combination, such as information, design concepts, etc.

Production—All operations or processes performed in the delivery of a finished product or service.

Put in Service—The stage at which a product is ready for use in the Community market for the first time for its intended purpose, after installation. For most products, this definition is being discontinued in favor of "placing on the market." It applies mainly to machinery and electrical equipment.

Qualification—The action of proving that any equipment or process works correctly and the output conforms to the EU requirements.

Quality Assurance—All those planned actions necessary to ensure that a product conforms to a certain level of quality.

Quality Control—The technique used to fulfill the requirements for quality.

Quality Manual—The document that states the quality policy, describes the quality system, and identifies the quality procedures and records.

Quality Plan—The document that sets out the specific quality practices, resources, and sequence of activities that will be carried out to ensure that a product or service meets the appropriate standards and directives.

Quality Record—The document that furnishes objective evidence of activities performed or results that demonstrate compliance.

Quality System—A set of procedures used to guarantee a minimum level of quality in a product. Normally defined in the directive and means ISO 9001/2/3 registration is required.

Quarantine—The status of a starting, intermediate, bulk, or finished material or product that is effectively separated from others until a decision is reached on its status (non-conforming product, material, or intermediate).

Recommendation—Reserved for EUROATOM. Equivalent to a directive.

Reconciliation—A management review in which a comparison is made between the theoretical amount of product or material used and the actual amount used. It takes into account statistical variations.

Recovery—The introduction of all or part of a previous batch into another batch, at a definite stage of production, so that the final quality meets standards. Also means that a product has been reworked to meet final quality standards.

Reference Standard—The value or sample used to compare against when calibrating measuring systems. It must be traceable to a known national standard.

Registered—When a company, location, or plant is certified for compliance to the appropriate standard after it has been audited by a Notified Body or registrar.

Registrar—An accredited third-party company that evaluates an organization to verify that its quality system is in compliance with the applicable standards.

Registration—Procedure by which a Notified Body indicates that an organization or person meets the required characteristics of a standard and then includes or registers the product, process, or service in an appropriate published and available list.

Regulated Product—A product that has important health, safety, or environmental implications, such as medical or personnel protection equipment.

Regulation—A community rule for implementing a specific directive, such as the regulation to set up the Medicinal Product Agency.

Reprocessing—The reworking of all or part of a non-conforming batch, from a definite stage of production, to make the final batch meet its Certificate of Conformity.

Return—The act of sending a product back to the manufacturer or distributor. It does not imply that there is a defect.

Rework—See *Reprocessing.*

Risks—The potential consequences of a process, procedure, or device failure.

Risks Assessment—A formal program to determine the potential outcome of different failure mechanisms.

Safeguard Clause—The article in a directive that grants the Member States the right to remove from the market any product which a Member State ascertains may compromise the health and/or safety of an EU citizen or of property.

Safety Component—A component, provided that it is not interchangeable equipment, which the manufacturer or his authorized representative within the Community places on the market to fulfill a safety function when in use and the failure or malfunctioning of which endangers the safety or health of exposed persons.

Safety Stop—The mechanism for emergency stopping of machinery to prevent injury.

Scheme—A certification procedure for products or a quality system designed by a specific EU country or standards organization.

Self-Certification—An official declaration by the manufacturer or service provider that the product meets the specific requirements of all relevant directives.

Serial Number—The unique number on a piece of equipment that identifies it. For example, for PEA equipment, the serial number must start with the letter D.

Signatory—The person who signs the Declaration of Conformity. He is responsible for placing a product on the market and is personally liable for the performance of the product or service.

Specifications—Clearly documented requirements and procedures which materials, bulk, and finished products must meet. Includes testing, work instructions, and process controls.

Standard—A technical specification written by a recognized standards body and approved by the EU Commission which a manufacturer must follow to be in compliance.

Standing Committee—A committee established by the EU to determine non-compliance of products and processes, approve standards and directives, and provide technical evaluations for the EU.

Statistical Verification—The process of using statistical procedures to ensure that a batch or continuous process is in compliance with its requirements.

STERILE—The EU symbol that indicates that a product is sterile.

Sterility—The absence of all living organisms.

Stop Control—A primary control that halts the movement of machinery and renders it safe.

Study Audit—A comparison of raw data with the final report to determine if the raw data were accurately reported. It also determines whether or not the testing was carried out correctly and whether it is necessary to obtain additional information regarding the validity of the testing.

Subcontractor—A person or company that supplies goods or services to a supplier.

Supplementary Protection Certificate—A certificate which extends the period of patent protection on medicinal products.

Supplier—The organization that provides a product or service.

Surveillance—The continuous monitoring and verification of procedures, products, and services to ensure that the requirements for quality are being met.

TAG—Abbreviation for Technical Advisory Group, which in a standards organization is responsible for developing any standard.

TCF—Abbreviation for Technical Construction File. See also *Technical Construction File.*

Technical Construction File (TCF)—Documentation prepared by a manufacturer or service provider which demonstrates compliance with EU Directives.

Technical Standard—The specific test methods or product specifications used to implement a directive.

Third Country—Any country that is not a member of the EU or the EEA.

Third Party—See *Registrar.*

TIF—Abbreviation for Technical Information File. Equivalent to TCF.

Traceability—A formal process of keeping track of the history and location of an item.

Transition Period—The time that elapses between the date a regulation or directive is passed until the Member States have transposed the requirements into national law. It is set in each directive.

Transparency—Access to information, as well as openness of operation and competition.

Type—A representative sample of a product or component. It can be a final or intermediate product.

Type-Examination—Either a harmonized test performed by the manufacturer or examination of the quality system by a Notified Body.

Unit Verification—The formal process of ensuring that an individual product is in compliance. It must be done by a Notified Body.

Validation—The formal act of proving that the process used leads to the expected result. It must be in accordance with the EU Directives.

Verification—The process of proving that a product meets its specific requirements under the EU Directives.

Vibration—The unwanted periodic moving of a piece or part of a machine which could affect its safe operation.

WG—Abbreviation for Work Group, which is a subcommittee of a TAG committee that develops the actual standards. For example, ISO TAG 212 on In-Vitro Diagnostic W2 on GLP.

Worker—Any person employed by an employer, including trainees and apprentices but excluding domestic servants.

Workers' Representative with Specific Responsibility for the Safety and Health of Workers—Any person elected, chosen, or designated in accordance with national laws and/or practices to represent workers when problems arise relating to protection of the safety and health of workers at work.

Worker's Safety Directives—A series of directives which most employers in the EU must follow. They guarantee that workers have a safe employment environment. A manufacturer or service provider who exports to the EU will probably have to meet these directives.

Working Coefficient—The arithmetic ratio between the load, as guaranteed by the manufacturer, to which a piece of equipment, an accessory, or machinery is able to hold up and the maximum working load marked on the equipment, accessory, or machinery.

References

Approximation of Taxes. Why? Office for Official Publications of the European Communities, Luxembourg, 1991 (Catalogue Number CC-73-91-368-EN-C).

The Citizens and the Single Market, Office for Official Publications of the European Communities, Luxembourg, 1995.

Creating Jobs, Office for Official Publications of the European Communities, Luxembourg, 1995 (Catalogue number CC-92-95-312-EN-C).

The EU AIMD (Active Implantable Medical Device) Directive, St. Lucie Press, Boca Raton, FL, 1997.

The EU Biocides Directives, St. Lucie Press, Boca Raton, FL, 1997.

EU Certification and Technical Standards Directives, St. Lucie Press, Boca Raton, The FL, 1997.

The EU Colorant Agents for Medicinal Product and Food Directives, St. Lucie Press, Boca Raton, FL, 1997.

The EU ECO-Label Directives, Regulations and Decisions, St. Lucie Press, Boca Raton, FL, 1997.

The EU Electro-Medical Equipment Directive, St. Lucie Press, Boca Raton, FL, 1997.

The EU EMC (Electromagnetic Compatibility) Directive, St. Lucie Press, Boca Raton, FL, 1997.

The EU EMEA (European Medicine Evaluation Agency) Regulations, St. Lucie Press, Boca Raton, FL, 1997.

The EU GCP (Guidelines for Good Clinical Practices): The Draft of the International Good Clinical Practices, St. Lucie Press, Boca Raton, FL, 1997.

The EU GLP (Good Laboratory Practices), St. Lucie Press, Boca Raton, FL, 1997.

The EU GMP (Good Manufacturing Practices), St. Lucie Press, Boca Raton, FL, 1997.

The EU Human Medicinal Products Directives, Opinions and Regulations, St. Lucie Press, Boca Raton, FL, 1997.

The EU Human Medicinal Products Testing Directives, St. Lucie Press, Boca Raton, FL, 1997.

The EU IVD: The Proposal for the In-Vitro Diagnostic Directive, St. Lucie Press, Boca Raton, FL, 1997.

The EU Labeling of Medicinal Product Directives, St. Lucie Press, Boca Raton, FL, 1997.

The EU Liability and Product Safety Directives, St. Lucie Press, Boca Raton, FL, 1997.

The EU Low Voltage Directive, St. Lucie Press, Boca Raton, FL, 1997.

The EU Machinery Directive, St. Lucie Press, Boca Raton, FL, 1997.

The EU MDD (Medical Device Directive), St. Lucie Press, Boca Raton, FL, 1997.

The EU Modules for Conformity Assessment Directives, St. Lucie Press, Boca Raton, FL, 1997.

The EU Packaging Directives, St. Lucie Press, Boca Raton, FL, 1997.

The EU PEA (Equipment Used in Potentially Explosive Atmospheres) Directive, St. Lucie Press, Boca Raton, FL, 1997.

The EU Risks Assessment: Directives and Regulations, St. Lucie Press, Boca Raton, FL, 1997.

The EU Special Medicinal Products Directives, St. Lucie Press, Boca Raton, FL, 1997.

The EU Veterinary Medicinal Product Testing Directives, St. Lucie Press, Boca Raton, FL, 1997.

The EU Video and Display Equipment Directive, St. Lucie Press, Boca Raton, FL, 1997.

The EU VMP (Veterinary Medicinal Products) Directives, St. Lucie Press, Boca Raton, FL, 1997.

The EU Worker's Safety: Physical Hazards Directive, St. Lucie Press, Boca Raton, FL, 1997.

The EU Worker's Safety: Work Equipment Directives, St. Lucie Press, Boca Raton, FL, 1997.

Europe in Ten Points, Office for Official Publications of the European Communities, Luxembourg, 1995.

The European Union and World Trade, Office for Official Publications of the European Communities, Luxembourg, 1995.

Freedom of Movement, Office for Official Publications of the European Communities, Luxembourg, 1995.

The Guide to the EU Institutions, Office for Official Publications of the European Communities, Luxembourg, 1995.

The Institutions of the European Union, Office for Official Publications of the European Communities, Luxembourg, 1995.

ISO 9000: Preparing for Registration, James L. Lamprecht, ASQC Quality Press, Marcel Dekker, Milwaukee, WI, 1992.

The ISO 9000 Documentation Tool Kit, Janet L. Novak, Prentice Hall P T R, Englewood Cliffs, NJ, 1994.

The ISO 9000 Handbook, Robert W. Peach (editor), Irwin Publishing, Fairfax, VA, 1992.

ISO Standards Compendium: ISO 9000 Quality Management, ISO, 1994.

Overview, Office for Official Publications of the European Communities, Luxembourg, 1996.

Protecting Our Environment, Office for Official Publications of the European Communities, Luxembourg, 1993 (Catalogue Number CC-77-93-853-EN-C).

The Single Market, Office for Official Publications of the European Communities, Luxembourg, 1993.

20 Questions and Answers: The Lome Convention between the European Community and the African, Caribbean, and Pacific States, Office for Official Publications of the European Communities, Luxembourg, 1996.

Index